Once Upon a Time in the Academic Library

Storytelling Skills for Librarians

edited by
Maria Barefoot, Sara Parme,
and Elin Woods

Association of College and Research Libraries
A division of the American Library Association
Chicago, Illinois 2022

The paper used in this publication meets the minimum requirements of American National Standard for Information Sciences–Permanence of Paper for Printed Library Materials, ANSI Z39.48-1992. ∞

Library of Congress Control Number: 2021952832

Copyright ©2022 by the Association of College and Research Libraries.

All rights reserved except those which may be granted by Sections 107 and 108 of the Copyright Revision Act of 1976.

Printed in the United States of America.

26 25 24 23 22 5 4 3 2 1

Contents

1   Introduction: The Roots of Storytelling in History, Theory, and Librarianship
Maria Barefoot, Elin Woods, and Sara Parme

Tales from the Information Literacy Classroom

27   Chapter 1. A Tale of Five Case Studies: Reflections on Piloting a Case-Based, Problem-Based Learning Curriculum in English Composition
Katie Strand, Rachel Wishkoski, Alex Sundt, and Deanna Allred

45   Chapter 2. Shooting for the Stars: Using a Story Ripped from the Astronomy Headlines with First-Year Students
Kathryn Yelinek

55   Chapter 3. Encouraging Connections: Using Personal Storytelling in the Information Literacy Classroom
Allyson Wind and Megan Smith

63   Chapter 4. The Moral of the Story Is… Appealing to Student Values in the Classroom
Gerald R. Natal

73   Chapter 5. Revealing the Means of (Information) Production: Collaborative Storytelling to Demystify Scholarship
Dunstan McNutt

Tales from the Stacks

93   Chapter 6. The Depository is Large. It Contains Multitudes
L. E. Eames

103 Chapter 7. Call and Response: Delicate Conversations in Collection Development
Alexis L. Pavenick

115 Chapter 8. Choose Your Own Path: Using Primary Sources and Oral History Interviews to Promote Life Experiences Found in Special Collections and University Archives
Harrison Wick

Tales from Physical and Virtual Library Spaces

123 Chapter 9. Let's Tell a Story: Narrative, Constructivism, and Accessibility
Anders Tobiason

133 Chapter 10. Using Existing Fandoms to Create Your Own Library Stories: How a Harry Potter-inspired Murder Mystery Introduced First-Year Students to the Library
Holly Jackson

157 Biographies

Introduction

The Roots of Storytelling in History, Theory, and Librarianship

Historical Roots of Storytelling

It could be argued that to tell stories is to be human. In fact, we as humans are wired for the sharing of stories.[1] We make sense of our world through them and some of us create entire professions out of a love of stories. As librarians, we are aware of the impact that stories have on our lives and our profession, but historically, stories have played a major role in our shared human development. "Storytelling is what we do in recounting our lives."[2] It is difficult to separate humanity from storytelling since it is "a defining characteristic of both human intelligence and our species,"[3] and is "an important human adaptation."[4] Stories have served humans throughout history in many ways

beyond simple entertainment or the passing on of knowledge. Sharing stories also plays a role in coordinating social behavior and promoting cooperation among groups of people.[5] Stories have been important for human survival and, as we will see later, sharing specific and more diverse kinds of stories are more important than ever before.

Humans are communal creatures and stories are our communal tools. In our need to communicate with one another, humans developed methods of sharing stories with one another. Without having another person to engage with, we lose both lessons and stories. "In an oral culture, the exchange of information requires at least two people, the speaker, and the listener, and is invariably a communal experience.... This group experience can build a common understanding and a sense of cohesion among listeners."[6] Sharing stories with one another also builds solidarity and stronger communities, providing opportunities for humans to work together to solve problems.[7] We can apply these developed problem-solving methods using storytelling to accomplish our shared goals because stories are truly never individual experiences once shared but become part of the collective.[8] If the problem is everyone's problem, more people are more likely going to work on solving what is ailing the community as a whole. Without stories, shared orally or written down, we as humans would not exist as we do today, nor would we have connections to one another.[9]

Definitions of Storytelling

Storytelling evolved alongside humans to provide entertainment in literature, plays, and visual arts. It helps shape society through parables, moral tales, and religion. Storytelling plays a role in business, law, medicine, and education in modern society. Each of these areas has a claim on the term storytelling and how it applies within these fields. Academic librarians can apply storytelling in the same way that teachers, entertainers, lawyers, and businesspeople have done for centuries. Within libraries, these definitions have fallen into two major categories thus far: storytelling as art during children's story hours and storytelling as education within information literacy instruction. This introduction explores both of these contexts as well as a broader definition of storytelling as communication, which librarians have begun to employ in the areas of reference, outreach, management, and assessment.

The earliest definitions of storytelling have focused on its use in art and literature. Vansina describes storytelling as cultural heritage using the spoken word.[10] Storytelling existed before written language existed or printed materials were widely distributed. Greek and Norse mythology were widely communicated as oral tales.[11] Before the written word, stories were communicated mainly through performance, either by a single storyteller or through staged performance in the ancient Greek traditions. Loy highlights how these mythologies were used to create a sense of community, examine moral situations, and explain the surrounding world. In this way, storytelling as art and performance pre-date science as the primary method for generating knowledge.[12] As printed language became more prevalent with the invention of the printing press, these mythologies were codified into formal versions of the informal oral traditions.

While this explanation of story is perhaps the most fundamental for human experiences, the reality of storytelling is that it has been applied in settings that expand well beyond art and literature. For instance, within education, storytelling is well-covered territory as a method of learning. While the natural fit for storytelling may feel like an elementary school reading lesson, teachers have used storytelling in all subjects, including math, science, and physical education.[13] In higher education, professors of medicine and law have discussed storytelling in their teaching practice as well.[14] Particularly in medicine, the use of scenarios is one of the primary teaching methods for new doctors and nurses. Students are confronted with complex patient situations in which they must make care decisions, communicate with patients and families, and diagnose diseases. All of these examples present storytelling as a pedagogical tool. Educators discuss storytelling as a method of sharing, retaining, and using information within the established curriculum. The important distinction here is that educators don't rely on telling a story in the hopes that students will understand and apply the message. Educators have changed storytelling from an art form into pedagogy when they ask students to make decisions based on information provided in various scenarios. This is often discussed in the education literature as problem-based learning, case-based learning, and narrative learning.

The broadest definition of storytelling comes from its applications in other areas of modern life. Shank highlights this when he asks his reader to imagine going through a day without telling a story to someone.[15] Think about the person that cut you off in traffic this morning, a big presentation that you nailed after it had been hanging over your head for weeks, or the moment when your child wanted to go to school dressed as their favorite superhero. We tell stories as a basic method of communicating our lives to those around us.

Academic librarians are situated in an amazing position to help students recognize larger stories through reference, instruction, collections, and archives. Early applications of storytelling in libraries came from children's librarians between the 1870s and 1890s.[16] These applications viewed storytelling as a form of entertainment similar to watching a live play, the difference being that a storyteller would use tone of voice and sometimes props or pictures to illustrate the story instead of dialogue, sets, and costumes. In the early 1900s, children's librarians at the Carnegie Library of Pittsburgh, Pratt Institute Free Library of Brooklyn, and the Buffalo Public Library were regularly offering children's storytelling programs.[17]

Even now, many librarians who hold a master's degree have taken a course in storytelling. Kate McDowell, who teaches such a course regularly, defines storytelling as "a practice involving a dynamic triangle of telling, listening, and story, drawing on both folklore and storytelling performance scholarship."[18] This view of storytelling leans heavily on the idea of storytelling as art. Other librarians have described assignments in such storytelling courses that involve locating stories such as folktales, social justice stories, and personal experiences. These assignments may include having library students tell the story in front of a group of people or via technology but almost always recommend that the student tell the story without using notes. These requirements echo those of storytelling organizations that mainly view stories as art and performance.[19]

As information literacy librarians entered the classroom in both academic and school environments, librarians began to employ storytelling as education. While one might argue that all art is education, the use of storytelling has expanded beyond the original artistic roots. As described earlier, educators have taken the art of storytelling and added pedagogical features that invite the viewer, listener, or student to apply their own knowledge and experiences to create new knowledge. Instruction librarians have done the same during information literacy sessions.

Vossler and Watts highlight how the *Framework for Information Literacy for Higher Education* relies on recognizing dispositions. Dispositions within the framework commonly refer to affective areas that drive our behaviors such as motivation and emotion.[20] These dispositions are well-suited for storytelling, and many librarians have described ways in which stories can be used in the classroom, such as student research journals, infographics, case studies, and role-playing. Badke points out that scholarship as conversation directly calls us to examine research as a narrative rather than a collection of facts.[21] All of these applications fall firmly within the realm of storytelling as education.

However, academic librarians are expanding these definitions daily into areas such as reference work, archival work, collection development, management, and assessment. These broader areas do not have as many examples available in the literature. However, they all fall firmly within the definition of storytelling as communication. While storytelling has been approached from an artistic, educative, and communicative stand in the literature, this book applies all three definitions at various stages. We take this approach because, just like storytelling, librarianship reaches across many disciplines. In order to use storytelling effectively, librarians must be able to apply the art behind it, understand the educational theories that support it, and communicate these stories clearly to a variety of audiences.

Theoretical Roots of Storytelling

While we are approaching storytelling as a communication method in this book, it's important to understand the theoretical roots of storytelling in all of its forms. Storytelling draws upon basic brain science to understand how humans learn, think, and adapt to situations. The three major theories we will examine include constructivism, affective learning theory, and narrative theory.

Constructivism

Constructivism as a theory was developed by three major theorists: Jean Piaget, Lev Vygotsky, and Ernst von Glasersfeld. Piaget developed the theory of cognitive constructivism, which asserts that humans build new knowledge upon prior knowledge.[22] In academic libraries, we often see this play out with students who are familiar with the natural language and algorithm-driven search mechanisms of Google. This prior knowledge leads students to apply the same search structure to keyword-driven library databases and catalogs. Library users who have relied on Google's search algorithm for many of the search queries they complete in their daily lives often assume that the strategies that were successful in that environment will be equally effective in other library interfaces, which is rarely the case.

Lev Vygotsky developed the idea of social constructivism, which asserts that we build knowledge based on our interactions with others.[23] His early work was carried out with children, but this same behavior can be seen in academic library spaces as well. Imagine a scenario where a library patron approaches the reference desk with an ISBN number for a book. This patron is likely building on their prior experiences interacting with salespeople at a bookstore or an online shopping site that can easily look up a book by an ISBN. So, when they hand the reference librarian the number, the librarian asks, "Do you know anything else about the book, like the author or title?" The patron's expression may shift to confusion, surprise, and frustration at being asked this question. In other social interactions, when searching for information, the ISBN has been all that was needed. This kind of scenario is a perfect example of how social interactions become vital in how a patron learns to use and interact with the library.

The third piece of constructivist theory is radical constructivism originally theorized by Ernst von Glasersfeld. In this theory of constructivism, he asserts that all knowledge is constructed rather than perceived through the senses.[24] Lisa Feldman Barrett has advanced this theory through her work on constructed emotion. She outlines how emotions are not universal experiences and are instead reliant upon the society in which they exist. With the exception of bad feelings and good feelings, humans experience emotions differently depending on the culture in which they are situated.[25] Jonathan Gottschall also discusses how this plays out with memory. Brain scientists have discovered that memories are fluid and change slightly every time we recall them.[26] Within libraries, we see this play out as we watch student workers or tour guides explain the library to prospective or new students. Without fail, student-led tours often emphasize one service in the library over another. Perhaps one tour guide mentions how they get all of their textbooks through interlibrary loan; this example shows how that student tour guide associated the library with that particular service that was helpful to them. Another student would likely emphasize something completely different in their own tours. The important piece to remember is that every student on that tour will likely find their own piece of the library to emphasize as they have their own experiences in the library. Radical constructivism recognizes that these experiences are unique to each student and each will remember their own experiences slightly differently.

These three theories of constructivism work together when we engage in storytelling. If we think back to the discussion of storytelling as an art, educational approach, and communication method, we can see all three of these approaches in constructivism as well. Palmer, Harshbarger, and Koch discuss the idea of fairy tales becoming learning devices, especially in children.[27] Fairy and folk tales are one of the best examples of how storytelling bridges the three definitions discussed earlier as well as rely on constructivism to enhance learning and communication. In fairy and folk tales, there is often a reliable structure to the story. The rhythm of the story becomes repetitive in a way that is easy for listeners to imitate and replicate. Constructivism as a whole recognizes that our brains must have a structure to create knowledge. That structure may be prior knowledge, experience, or memory, but the result is that we build knowledge from previous moments in our lives, which makes every learning experience learning unique to the learner.

Affective Learning Theory

Like constructivism, affective learning theory builds on how the brain naturally works to create new knowledge. Affective learning theory acknowledges the role that emotion, attitudes, and motivation play in creating new knowledge. Affective learning theory refers to one of three educational domains outlined by Benjamin Bloom, David Krathwhol, and Bertram B. Masia, which included the cognitive, affective, and psychomotor domains of learning.[28] The affective domain specifically consists of five categories: receiving, responding, valuing, organizing, and characterizing.

Each of these categories builds on the previous one to work toward internalizing new information. When someone internalizes new information, it begins to guide and change their behavior. At the beginning stage of receiving, the learner is simply aware of new information. At the responding stage, the learner must engage with the new information. Information literacy librarians who are aware of active learning pedagogy will recognize the responding stage as a common way to incorporate active learning into instruction sessions. The last three categories, however, are harder to measure and incorporate because they rely on the learner to engage with the material. In the valuing category, learners must be able to see and express how that piece of information is valuable to their own goals. Organizing involves combining values, information, and ideas and relating them to previously held beliefs. Valuing and organizing may sound familiar from the discussion of constructivism. In these stages, the learner must find ways to relate information to their own lives and place value on that information. The final category of characterizing is where learners have internalized new information and begun to form new behaviors around that information.

With these stages in mind, let's think back to the scenario of the student with an ISBN number at the reference desk. In order to adjust their behavior in a library setting, the student will not only have to receive the information that they can't use the ISBN to search for a book, but they will also have to respond to that knowledge, find value in the result, organize that piece of information alongside the existing knowledge they have about searching for textbooks, and then categorize it so that it becomes a part of their regular behavior. The process is ripe with emotional cracks that would cause students to steer clear of the library in the future. For example, the student may be willing to learn the library structure in the responding category but finds that the library doesn't have the book they were looking for. At this point, the student may have trouble valuing the new information.

One of the major benefits of using storytelling pedagogy in academic library settings is that storytelling has evolved to include the affective domain. The use of emotion in storytelling is one of the major ways that we relate to characters and situations. Lisa Cron describes how stories rely on emotion when she says that effective stories only include information that affects the protagonist in some way. The protagonist has opinions about the events in a plot, he or she gets angry, confused, or frustrated depending on what has happened to them.[29] The human brain has the impressive ability to re-create emotional responses from stories as if we were actually living those emotions.[30] While telling a story is an excellent way of evoking emotion and engaging the affective learning dimension in our students, an even better way is to ask students to tell their own stories. This is exactly the kind of storytelling that narrative theory addresses.

Narrative Theory

Narrative Theory is the study of how people construct and use stories to make meaning out of events. Narrative theory is, in fact, the basis of story as a communication method. While affective learning theory and constructivist theories developed within educational and social environments, narrative theory was developed by Walter Fisher as a way of explaining human communication.[31] Narrative theory clashes with the rational world paradigm by questioning the idea that humans make decisions based on logic. Rather, narrative theory claims that humans make decisions based on narrative rationality, which is determined by how accurately our own experiences reflect those of the story that we are presented with. Fisher called this concept narrative fidelity.

With these ideas in mind, we can see how narrative theory builds on social constructivism. Humans must recognize their own experiences within a story in order to build from that story. We can also see how affective learning theory comes into play by asking the reader or listener to internalize the story as they generate their own meaning from it. Cron discusses how narratives do not just exist to entertain or even to organize information. Instead, they exist as a way for our brains to identify and solve problems.[32]

If we approach the idea of seeking information from a narrative perspective, we can recognize that, for students, reference questions and research papers are often situated within a particular problem. Badke highlights this by saying that all researchers bring stories of fear, procrastination, curiosity, and relationships to their research process.[33] In order to access this internal narrative, Detmering and Johnson advocate for having students reflect on their research narrative in information literacy instruction. In their research, they often found that students felt discouraged when they were asked to minimize their own voices in their research and that students found research tasks most rewarding when they were asked to reflect on their own assumptions and values surrounding the research process.[34] While their research focused on the information literacy classroom, it could also be applied at service points throughout the library as well as being embedded in the reference interview.

As we will learn in the next section, stories rely on a few vital components, including sympathetic characters, problems that contribute to the plot, and emotional engagement as the characters work toward a solution to the problems they encounter. In this way, stories are essentially a problem-solving exercise for our brains.

The Mechanics of Storytelling

As we have already examined, storytelling relies not only on the existence of a story that may be told by a librarian or examined by a student but also on the previous experiences, affective domain, and narrative that the patron is experiencing in relation to that story. Lipman suggests that storytelling encompasses three entities: the teller, the listener, and the story itself.[35] Therefore, as librarians craft stories for use in their work, they should consider how the plot, conflict, and characterization reflect the information they wish to convey as well as how it may be received by the patron. When constructing a story, curiosity is key. Lisa Cron suggests asking yourself these questions when constructing a story: Whose story is it? What is happening? and What's at stake?[36] It's important that the librarian approach these questions from the perspective of the patron rather than a librarian.

Thuna and Szurmak studied how information literacy librarians use storytelling in their classrooms. Their interviews showed a few major themes, such as librarians providing anecdotes, metaphors, and using storytelling to explain processes. Within these themes, there were also sub-themes, which included case studies, verbal vignettes, active learning, and aligning stories with the ACRL *Framework for Information Literacy for Higher Education*.[37] The mechanics of an effective story within librarianship relies on how librarians portray the characters and situations in these vignettes, case studies, etc.

For instance, case studies themselves have been discussed as scenario-based learning, case-based learning, and problem-based learning. Each of these uses storytelling as a basis for asking students to apply knowledge to situations. In my research, I experimented with problem-based learning and storytelling when I asked my students to read real stories from the website Humans of New York, identify possible information needs, and then identify how the person in the story might satisfy that need.[38] These stories were never intended for use in a library classroom, but the stories came from real people with real problems. This is one of the hallmarks of effective storytelling. The situation that the characters find themselves in must feel real to the patron. In the Humans of New York example, students were asked to place themselves within someone else's situation to identify an information need. This was uncomfortable for many of them since there was no clear answer to the problem.

Anne Lamott suggests in her book, *Bird by Bird*, that it is common for people to try to write what they know in terms of plot or events; however, it is much more effective to write what you know to be true emotionally.[39] As librarians construct stories for use in instructional settings, in online materials, and through interactions with patrons, we must ask ourselves, what would a patron feel when presented with this material? Then, strive to include those feelings through the use of descriptive emotional language. The brain processes emotion words as though we were actually feeling them.[40] This means that by including emotion words in our own storytelling, we are both acknowledging patron experiences and helping them navigate those experiences to use the library more effectively. It is tempting to remove all emotion from professional writing, teaching, and interactions in an effort to seem more authoritative on any given subject. However, the removal of emotional language also means that our patrons may struggle to find their own experiences reflected in the stories we tell.

While emotional language is important, it is also vital that we consider the actions that each character takes as part of a larger plot. Detmering and Johnson have studied student research narratives and, according to their research, students often see themselves as heroes, failures, or rebels. Alternatively, they also represent their teachers in a number of ways, including nurturers and buffoons.[41] While librarians were not included in this study, it is reasonable to expect that we also play into their mental narrative of writing academic papers or seeing information. When librarians interact with patrons, we should consider ourselves entering that existing narrative. The reference interview is an excellent place to figure out how librarians can step into a research narrative. Did the student describe their assignment as something they "have to get done?" In this scenario, the librarian could become an unwelcome figure if the library doesn't own the materials the student needs. They may become exasperated at being told they'll need to wait a few days for an interlibrary loan item to arrive. While this scenario may be frustrating for all parties involved, it could provide excellent materials for developing scenarios for use in class or in online learning materials.

In order to identify and build upon these naturally occurring library-related plots, Palmer, Harshbarger, and Koch suggest the use of story maps. Their research focused on young children, but they employed the use of story maps to help students understand and build on existing stories. In story mapping, a professional storyteller asked children to create a story from a series of images.[42] By asking patrons to share their experiences of research through written or visual storytelling, librarians can allow those stories to take on a life of their own that helps new users to create their own research narratives. While the most obvious applications of such a technique are in the library classroom, student research narratives could be shared on library websites or with administrators as part of advocating for the library. Additionally, faculty research narratives could help build relationships where none existed previously. In short, storytelling is a method for academic librarians to reach out to the larger community and situate ourselves as key characters in their academic lives.

Even as we begin to build these narratives with the help of library patrons, it is imperative that librarians understand that many times the voices we encounter will not come from cultures, ethnicities, socioeconomic statuses, or gender identities that conform to those of the librarians that they engage with. This reality makes it imperative that librarians understand and respect the narratives of their patrons.

Social Justice Applications

As was explored previously, storytelling serves as a tool for creating better teams and allowing for better communication with one another. Stories and storytelling techniques can be used to create a better future for all of us by considering the ways that stories have been used in the past while also exploring whose stories have been told and whose have not in the present day. The upcoming submitted pieces by contributing authors all include a section titled "Cultural Considerations." These sections required the authors to consider ways that they were or were not using examples outside of their own space. It also presented them with an opportunity to think about including aspects of social justice within their already existing work to share with readers of this book. Real-world applications of this work will be shared in each submitted chapter.

As librarians, we use stories on a daily basis. When we share examples in our classrooms, when we market our services to our students, even when we put up displays in our buildings, we are sharing a story and are directing the narrative. Directing the narrative is something very linked in the history of librarianship in the United States. As one of the accepted "founders" of librarianship in the United States, Melvil Dewey formatted librarianship in a similar structure to that of Christian missionary work. Using "the language of Christianity as a rhetorical device," early librarians often worked in communities teaching, especially children, how to better themselves through books and better fit into the majority of the population.[43] Looking at the statistics of today's contemporary librarians, it is easy to notice that there is a distinct racial majority within the field and that majority therefore controls the stories that are told. A survey conducted by the American Library Association in 2012, titled Diversity Counts, showed that 88 percent of librarians are white.[44] This is not something new within librarianship nor has much changed over the years, unfortunately. An earlier Diversity Counts survey showed just a one percent increase in librarians of color over the course of two years.

When people think about libraries, they think of books. They are certainly not our only tools, but they are still the common element when thinking of our buildings and our work. The telling of stories to promote emergent literacy in young children was one of the original roles that storytelling held in libraries.[45] The use of books as a tool to accomplish this meant that specific stories were shared with children, much like the materials we use today are shared with our students and campuses. In 1965, Nancy Larrick shocked the world with her article "The All-White World of Children's Books." Her findings surrounding children's literature at the time showed an evident lack of diversity, focusing solely on the lack of portrayals of Black Americans in children's books. "Out of 5,206 books published between the years of 1962–1964, only 6.7 percent of the books she explored included one or more Black characters, and less than 1 percent included contemporary portrayals. Most of the books were historical depictions. There seems to be little chance of developing the humility so urgently needed for world cooperation ...as long as children are brought up on gentle doses of racism through their books."[46]

To look at this algebraically, if most books in the library hold white characters' stories, the library must be a space for only real-life white characters. Unfortunately, the stories shared in books, focusing on publishing trends, does little to shift the narrative and create spaces for other voices in libraries. According to the 2010 Census, there are currently 74.2 million children under eighteen in the United States, with nearly half—46 percent—being children of color and Indigenous children. Additionally, today more than one-fifth of America's children are immigrants or children of immigrants. However, the books being published for this audience have not kept up with the cultural and racial population trends. "In 2011, the CCBC (Cooperative Children's Book Center) received approximately 3,400 books; of those, only 8.8 percent were multicultural."[47] One hundred and twenty-three books had significant African or African American content; twenty-eight books had American Indian themes, topics, or characters; ninety-one books had significant Asian/Pacific or Asian/Pacific American content, and fifty-eight books had significant Latino content.[48] This means that only one book out of every ten books has been written for children not centering whiteness. If we look at the Diversity Baseline Survey, conducted in 2019, the publishing industry remains just as white as ever. Like librarians, those who are deciding which books are being published are from the dominant culture. This means we need to actively seek ways to incorporate other stories in our work.[49] On a perhaps bright note, however, the survey did find that nearly half of the interns in the industry were from racial minority groups, showing potential change.

As we have seen, in the nearly fifty years between Larrick's findings and the current data, little has changed within libraries and publishing, while outside the world is changing; we are just not keeping up with it. Our students are coming to campus with an understanding that the library has books, and most of them do not understand them or make them feel like they belong in our buildings. So, what can we do and how can we create spaces where they do belong, while also contributing to greater change in the world? One quite simple answer: storytelling.

It has been written that only good stories survive.[50] But who is deciding what is a good story today and who has been deciding what stories have been good throughout history? This brings up an important topic of conversation within storytelling connected to dominant cultures and colonization. When European settlers colonized what is now the United States, the Indigenous peoples already living here had their own stories and histories. Yet because they were not something understood by Europeans, they were declared "a people without enlightenment, as a people without history," and therefore easily erased, which continues to this day.[51] Daniel Heath Justice contends that while there are good stories shared about Indigenous peoples, others, however, most often shared from outside of the community are not so good at all. Referring to these stories as "Indigenous deficiency," Justice shares how these dominant cultures have continually directed the narrative about marginalized communities from the beginning.[52] This is a recognizable trend throughout the history of both academia and libraries.

As noted earlier, libraries and librarians have largely been sharing stories using both the materials that are available to them and from their own experiences. Clearly, there is a bias, even if unintentional, in what is being shared. According to the work of Solorzano and Yosso, stories told by the dominant culture, which is white and therefore centering whiteness, are known as majoritarian stories. These types of stories are defined as a "bundle of presuppositions, perceived wisdoms, and shared cultural understanding persons in the dominant race bring to the discussion of race."[53] Majoritarian stories distort and silence the experiences of people of color and often "tells us that darker skin and poverty correlate with bad neighborhoods and bad schools…informs us that limited or Spanish-accented English and Spanish surnames equal bad schools and poor academic performance…reminds us that people who may not have the legal documents to 'belong' in the United

States may be identified by their skin color, hair texture, eye shape, accent, and/or surname."[54] We know that 88 percent of all librarians are white, so therefore we could safely assume that the stories being told, even if unintentional, are majoritarian in nature. This means that the stories being passed on to our library patrons are those from dominant Western cultures. Librarians are sharing and telling stories with bias, and we are telling them to an ever-increasingly diverse group of students on our campuses. According to projected numbers, "the United States is projected to become a majority nonwhite nation in 2043. While the non-Hispanic white population will remain the largest single group, no group will make up a majority."[55] For this reason, among many others, we should be fully committed to seeking ways to decrease the bias in the stories we share.

There is another form of storytelling, however, that can help work against majoritarian stories. This type of story is known as the counter-story or counter-storytelling. "Counter-storytelling is defined by critical race theory scholars as a method of telling the stories of those people whose experiences are not often told, including people of color, the poor, and members of the LGBTQ community. Counter-stories challenge the stereotypes often held by the dominant culture, give voice to marginalized youth, and present the complexity of racial and ethnic identity formation."[56] Counter-stories challenge what Adiche defines as "the single story."[57] Single stories rely on stereotypes, often the most negative, to portray one-dimensional characters throughout various media forms. The single story perpetuates the stereotype and leaves the majoritarian culture with notions of this being the reality of these groups. If those are the tales they are confronted with, those become the stories that are passed along and turn into history. This causes majoritarian cultures to view minority groups in deficit terms.[58] Bell furthers the topic of using counter-stories by breaking stories into four different categories: stock stories, which are similar to single/majoritarian stories and help reinforce privilege and the status quo, concealed stories, resistance stories, and emerging/transforming stories.[59] Exploring these last three types of stories, sharing the information known about these stories, and using them in our work is vital to creating social justice in libraries as they form the backbone of the counter-story.

What counter-stories do in turn then is to reshape and reframe the narrative. Utilizing counter-stories is beneficial for everyone, according to Richard

Delgado. They help those who do not fit into the majoritarian culture by giving them a voice to tell their own stories; therefore, "they gain healing from becoming familiar with their historical oppression and victimization; realize that they are not alone; that others have had the same thoughts and experiences; stop blaming themselves for their marginal position; construct additional counter-stories to challenge the dominant story."[60] But counter-stories also help those in the majoritarian culture to "overcome their ethnocentrism and the unthinking conviction that their way of seeing the world is the only one—that the way things are is inevitable, natural, and best."[61] However, it is important to note that counter-stories are not fictionalized characters and accounts but are rather "creating 'composite' characters grounded in real-life experiences and empirical data, not based on a fictional narrative or reality."[62] By actively choosing to reframe the narrative around our students in positive and supportive ways, we can in turn reframe the narrative around the library as a place where all may feel welcome.

We can start with ourselves and be honest with our students about who we are and how we hold space in libraries. "An integral part of good teaching …is the use of storytelling, which enables faculty to reveal their identities to students, bridge the divide too often secured by status, and provide them with opportunities to learn by grasping concepts from real life situations to which they can relate."[63] In an article published in the *Chronicle*, Justin Quarry does this by sharing his experience of "coming out of the closet as working class," allowing him to share his experiences in his classroom and inform his students that he understood their particular struggles because they had been his own.[64] Sharing stories in this way also allows librarians to further explore the role that privilege has both in academic spaces and what privileges they hold as individuals. Consider Peggy McIntosh's "Invisible Knapsack" exercise.[65] McIntosh confronts white privilege in her now-famous exploration of the conditions of her non-white colleagues. She challenges her fellow white peers to examine the ways in which they carry a knapsack full of the necessary tools to guide their way to success. If we return to the statistical makeup of librarians, there seems to be a lot of these knapsacks and privilege in the field. While librarians should share their personal stories and make connections, they should also hold space for their more marginalized peers and their students.

Collaborating with students in the reframing and reshaping of how we use stories is an excellent approach to fostering that space for the sharing of stories. Connecting to our students on real levels, moving away from classical learning approaches, where the instructor wields all the power in the room, and rather turn to constructivist approaches, we as librarians can "shift the dynamics in the classroom to empower students."[66] Empowering students gives them opportunities to use their voices, create those counter-stories, and maybe even entrust us to help share them. Sharing stories can be done in classrooms and while supporting a student at the reference desk. We should regularly be looking at the ways that we can bring back the human element into our services and into our buildings. Sharing stories is creating community.

Another approach that can be used in making strides toward social justice in libraries is micro-activism.[67] Creating change in our library spaces does not have to mean grand acts but can be done in small ways, bringing other people to the cause, and tackling the problems as a group, rather than as a single person. Remember the historical purposes of storytelling and community building? Acts of micro-activism can easily turn into larger movements of macro-activism, but we must start somewhere. Creating book displays is an easy way to deliver a message and share a story with our patrons. These displays speak to the collections we have in our libraries and what voices we consider worthwhile to have in our collections. Following advice from Morales, Knowles, and Bourg, "academic librarians must actively and aggressively collect resources by and about underrepresented groups."[68] We should also consider questions such as these: Who are we partnering with when we create programming? Are we asking people to come to us or are we proactively going out into our campus communities and seeking organizations that have long been marginalized? Are we considering all the students on our campuses? If we do not, what messages are we sending from the library?

While moving toward the goal of an antiracist library should be of our utmost priority; racial diversity and divides are not the only elements that librarians should consider when exploring social justice applications of storytelling. Alluded to earlier, we should also consider other aspects like class, gender, sexuality, exceptionalities, and culture. Librarians can create change on campuses but must do it by interacting with those from various backgrounds. Rather than share only majoritarian or single stories, librarians should actively seek out ways to include multiple voices when sharing stories by seeking out ways to reframe narratives and using counter-stories as often as possible in their work.

The work of social justice will not happen overnight, but that does not mean we should not all take the first steps today toward this goal. Much like keeping the art of storytelling alive, we all have a part to play in this mission. Together, using our shared experiences and making sure that we are all sharing stories in equal measure, we can accomplish great things. Stories have supported human survival, and they will continue to do so as long as they are viewed as powerful tools at one's disposal and used for the benefit of the many no longer just the few. The act of storytelling and libraries have a long-shared history, and as librarians seek to create the libraries of the future, returning to stories is an excellent way to build a solid foundation.

Librarian Storytelling Approaches

The chapter authors in this book have all endeavored to use storytelling to share diverse viewpoints that connect with their patrons. The practical examples at the end of each chapter illustrate how storytelling can be used within the academic library, and the chapters have been grouped by areas of library service. Notably, many of the chapters focus on using storytelling during information literacy instruction sessions. This is not surprising given that this is the arena where librarians have the most control over interactions with students and faculty. It is also indicative of the pedagogical developments that mirror storytelling, such as case-based learning, problem based-learning, journaling, and reflective teaching.

However, the theoretical basis of storytelling has also shown other ways that storytelling can be employed as a communication method. The other sections of this book include examples of how storytelling has been used as a communication method in sharing and developing collections, at service points, and in online spaces. These chapters are sparser than those focusing on storytelling as a pedagogical tool. However, these are the exact areas where the constructivist, narrative and affective theories come into play most often.

For example, Sara Parme and Elin Woods used storytelling in their outreach effort to learn more about how students feel about the cost of textbooks which was then used to inform an outreach effort on using open educational resources. They provided a whiteboard, pens, and Post-it notes in a public area of the library and asked students to leave their opinions on the cost of textbooks and the amount they had spent that semester on their textbooks. The answers they received tapped into all three of these theories by giving them a window into the student research narrative, their affective domain, and the background experiences that led them to develop those opinions. They were able to use those Post-it-sized stories in communications with faculty, campus administration, and library staff.[69] This example provides a window into the multitude of ways that librarians can use stories and storytelling theory in their everyday work.

Absent from this book are chapters on using storytelling within library management and assessment. These are areas that are ripe for development along with the less explored areas of using storytelling at library service points and in collections. We hope that the stories described in these chapters inspire you to invent new ways of using storytelling in your own library work.

Endnotes

1. Renate Chancellor and Shari Lee, "Storytelling: Oral History and Building the Library Community," *Storytelling, Self, Society: Storytelling in Libraries* 12, no. 12 (2016): 39, https://doi.org/10.13110/storselfsoci.12.1.0039.
2. Howard Woodhouse, "Storytelling in University Education: Emotion, Teachable Moments, and the Value of Life," *The Journal of Educational Thought* 45, no. 3 (2011): 213, https://www.jstor.org/stable/23767205.
3. John Terrell, "Storytelling and Prehistory," *Archaeological Method and Theory* 2 (1990): 2, https://www.jstor.org/stable/20170203.
4. Daniel Smith, Philip Schlaepfer, Katie Major, Mark Dyble, et al., "Cooperation and the Evolution of Hunter-Gatherer Storytelling," *Nature Communications* 8 (2017): 2, https://www.nature.com/articles/s41467-017-02036-8.
5. Smith, Schlaepfer, Major, Dyble, et al., "Cooperation and the Evolution, 3.
6. Chancellor and Lee, "Storytelling: Oral History," 40.
7. Woodhouse, "Storytelling in University Education," 216.
8. Patricia Ewick and Susan S. Silbey, "Subversive Stories and Hegemonic Tales: Toward a Sociology of Narrative," *Law & Society Review* 29, no. 2 (1995): 200, https://doi.org/10.1086/378035.
9. Chancellor and Lee, "Storytelling: Oral History," 41.
10. Jan Vansina, *Oral Tradition as History* (Madison, WI: University of Wisconsin Press), 93.
11. David Adams Leeming, *Storytelling Encyclopedia, Historical, Cultural, and Multiethnic Approaches to Oral Traditions Around the World* (Phoenix, AZ: The Oryx Press), 13.

12. David Loy, *The World is Made of Stories* (Boston, MA: Wisdom Publications), 59.
13. William Mooney and David Holt, *The Storyteller's Guide: Storytellers Share Advice for the Classroom, Boardroom, Showroom, Podium, Pulpit, and Center Stage* (Little Rock, AR: August House), 141.
14. Donna M. Steslow and Carolyn Gardner, "More Than One Way to Tell a Story: Integrating Storytelling into Your Law Course," *Journal of Legal Studies Education* 28, no. 2 (2011): 249, https://doi.org/10.1111/j.1744-1722.2011.01091.x
15. Roger C. Schank, *Tell Me a Story: Narrative and Intelligence* (Evanston, IL: Northwestern University Press), 7.
16. Kate McDowell, "Storytelling: Practice and Process as Non-Textual Pedagogy," *Education for Information* 34, no. 1 (2018): 15, https://doi.org/10.3233/EFI-189003.
17. Kay Bishop and Melanie A. Kimball, "Engaging Students in Storytelling," *Teacher Librarian* 33, no. 4 (2006): 28, http://thegatheringteachers.weebly.com/uploads/3/2/1/0/32109417/eci_808_storytelling.pdf.
18. McDowell, "Storytelling: Practice and Process," 16.
19. "What is Storytelling?," National Storytelling Network, accessed February 12, 2021, https://storynet.org/what-is-storytelling/.
20. Joshua J. Vossler and John Watts, "Educational Story as a Tool for Addressing the Framework for Information Literacy for Higher Education," *portal: Libraries and the Academy* 17, no. 3 (2017): 529, https://doi.org/10.1353/pla.2017.0033.
21. William Badke, "Research Is a Narrative," *Online Searcher* 39, no. 1 (2015): 70.
22. Jacqueline Grennon Brooks, "Constructivism," in *Encyclopedia of Cognitive Science*, ed. L. Nadel (New York: Wiley, 2005), https://onlinelibrary.wiley.com/doi/book/10.1002/0470018860.
23. Brooks, "Constructivism."
24. Brooks, "Constructivism."
25. Lisa Feldman Barrett, *How Emotions are Made* (New York: Houghton Mifflin Harcourt Publishing Company, 2017), 128.
26. Jonathan Gottschall, *The Storytelling Animal: How Stories Make Us Human* (New York: Houghton Mifflin Harcourt Publishing Company, 2012), 164.
27. Barbara C. Palmer, Shelley J. Harshbarger, and Cindy A. Koch, "Storytelling as a Constructivist Model for Developing Language and Literacy," *Journal of Poetry Therapy* 14 (2001): 199, https://doi.org/10.1023/A:1017541527998.
28. David R. Krathwohl, Benjamin S. Bloom, and Bertram B. Masia, *Taxonomy of Educational Objectives, the Classification of Educational Goals. Handbook II: Affective Domain* (New York: David McKay Co, Inc., 1964).
29. Lisa Cron, *Wired for Story: The Writer's Guide to Using Brain Science to Hook Readers from the Very First Sentence* (New York: Ten Speed Press, 2012), 47.
30. Will Storr, *The Science of Storytelling: Why Stories Make Us Human and How to Tell Them Better*, read by the author, audiobook, 7 hr., 3 min. (New York: HarperCollins Publishers, 2019).
31. James Watson and Anne Hill, "Narrative paradigm," *Dictionary of Media and Communication Studies*, 9th ed. (New York: Bloomsbury Publishing, 2015).
32. Cron, *Wired for Story*, 8.
33. Badke, "Research Is a Narrative," 70.
34. Robert Detmering and Anna Marie Johnson, "'Research Papers Have Always Seemed Very Daunting': Information Literacy Narratives and the Student Research Experience," *portal: Libraries and the Academy* 12, no. 1 (2012): 5–22, https://doi.org/10.1353/pla.2012.0004.

35. Doug Lipman. *Improving Your Storytelling: Beyond the Basics for All Who Tell Stories in Work or Play* (Little Rock, AR: August House, 1999).
36. Cron, *Wired for Story*, 19.
37. Joanna Szurmak and Mindy Thuna, "Tell Me a Story: The Use of Narrative as Tool for Instruction," in *Imagine, Innovate, Inspire: The Proceedings of the ACRL 2013 Conference*, ed. D. M. Mueller (2013), American Library Association, http://www.ala.org/acrl/sites/ala.org.acrl/files/content/conferences/confsandpreconfs/2013/papers/Szurmak-Thuna_TellMe.pdf.
38. Maria R. Barefoot, "Identifying Information Need through Storytelling," *Reference Services Review* 46 No. 2 (2018): 251–63, https://doi.org/10.1108/RSR-02-2018-0009.
39. Anne Lamott, *Bird by Bird* (New York: Anchor Books, 1995), 54.
40. Wayne R. Cherry, Jr., "Our Place in the Universe: The Importance of Story and Storytelling in the Classroom," *Knowledge Quest* 46, no. 2 (2017): 50.
41. Detmering and Johnson, "'Research Papers Have Always Seemed Very Daunting.'"
42. Palmer, Harshbarger, and Koch, "Storytelling as a Constructivist Model," 199–212.
43. Christine Pawley, "Unequal Legacies: Race and Multiculturalism in the LIS Curriculum," *The Library Quarterly: Information, Community, Policy* 76, no. 2 (2006): 155, https://doi.org/10.1086/506955.
44. "Diversity Counts," American Library Association, accessed January 11, 2021, http://www.ala.org/aboutala/offices/diversity/diversitycounts/divcounts.
45. Chancellor and Lee, "Storytelling: Oral History," 41.
46. Sandra Hughes-Hassell, "Multicultural Young Adult Literature as a Form of County-Storytelling," *The Library Quarterly: Information, Community, Policy* 83, no. 3 (2013): 212, https://doi.org/10.1086/670696.
47. Hughes-Hassell, "Multicultural Young Adult Literature," 213.
48. Ibid.
49. "Where is the Diversity in Publishing? The 2019 Diversity Baseline Survey Results," *The Open Book Blog* (blog), Lee & Low Books, January 28, 2020, https://blog.leeandlow.com/2020/01/28/2019diversitybaselinesurvey/.
50. Brian W. Strum and Sarah Beth Nelson, "What Can Folktales Teach Us about Higher Education Teaching?," *Storytelling, Self, Society* 13, no. 2 (2017): 171, https://digitalcommons.wayne.edu/storytelling/vol13/iss2/3.
51. Ashley Edwards, "Unsettling the Future by Uncovering the Past: Decolonizing Academic Libraries and Librarianship," *Partnership: The Canadian Journal of Library and Information Practice and Research* 14, no. 1 (2019): 3, https://journal.lib.uoguelph.ca/index.php/perj/article/view/5161.
52. Daniel Heath Justice, *Why Indigenous Literatures Matter* (Waterloo, Ontario: Wilfrid Laurier University Press, 2018), 23–24.
53. Daniel G. Solorzano and Tara J. Yosso, "Critical Race Methodology: Counter-Storytelling as an Analytical Framework for Education Research," *Qualitative Inquiry* 8, no. 1 (2002): 28, https://doi.org/10.1177/107780040200800103.
54. Solorzano and Yosso, "Critical Race Methodology," 29.
55. Myrna Morales, Em Claire Knowles, and Chris Bourg, "Diversity, Social Justice, and the Future of Libraries," *portal: Libraries and the Academy* 14, no. 3 (2014): 442, https://doi.org/10.1353/pla.2014.0017.
56. Solorzano and Yosso, "Critical Race Methodology," 32; Hughes-Hassell, "Multicultural Young Adult Literature," 12.

57. Chimamanda Ngozi Adichie, "The Danger of a Single Story," filmed July 2009 in Oxford, England. TED video, 18:26, https://www.ted.com/talks/chimamanda_ngozi_adichie_the_danger_of_a_single_story.
58. Hughes-Hassell, "Multicultural Young Adult Literature," 216.
59. Lee Anne Bell and Rosemarie A. Roberts, "The Storytelling Project Model: A Theoretical Framework for Critical Examination of Racism Through the Arts," *Teachers College Record* 112, no. 9 (2010): 2309–13, https://www.researchgate.net/publication/265758206_The_Storytelling_Project_Model_A_Theoretical_Framework_for_Critical_Examination_of_Racism_Through_the_Arts.
60. Richard Delgado, "Storytelling for Oppositionists and Others: A Plea for Narrative," *Michigan Law Review Association* 87, no. 8 (1989): 2437, https://doi.org/10.2307/1289308.
61. Hughes-Hassell, "Multicultural Young Adult Literature," 215.
62. Solorzano and Yosso, "Critical Race Methodology," 36.
63. Woodhouse, "Storytelling in University Education," 218–19.
64. Justin Quarry, "Coming Out as Working Class," *The Chronicle of Higher Education* (October 25, 2018), https://www.chronicle.com/article/coming-out-as-working-class/.
65. Peggy McIntosh, "White Privilege: Unpacking the Invisible Knapsack," *Peace and Freedom Magazine* (July/August 1989): 10–12, https://nationalseedproject.org/about-us/white-privilege.
66. Strum and Nelson, "What Can Folktales Teach Us," 189.
67. Rachel Lockman, "Academic Librarians and Social Justice: A Call to Microactivism," *College & Research Libraries News* 76, no. 4 (2015), https://crln.acrl.org/index.php/crlnews/article/view/9292/10372#b5-0760193.
68. Morales, Knowles, and Bourg, "Diversity, Social Justice, and the Future of Libraries," 446.
69. Elin Woods and Sara Parme, "Fight the Power: Giving Voice to Student Concerns About Textbook Prices," lecture, SSHELCO Virtual Conference, April 10, 2020.

Bibliography

Adichie, Chimamanda Ngozi. "The Danger of a Single Story." Filmed July 2009, Oxford, England. TED video, 18:26. https://www.ted.com/talks/chimamanda_ngozi_adichie_the_danger_of_a_single_story.

American Library Association. "Diversity Counts." Accessed January 11, 2021. http://www.ala.org/aboutala/offices/diversity/diversitycounts/divcounts.

Badke, William. "Research Is a Narrative." *Online Searcher* 39, no. 1 (2015): 68–70.

Barefoot, Maria R. "Identifying Information Need through Storytelling." *Reference Services Review* 46 No. 2 (2018): 251–63. https://doi.org/10.1108/RSR-02-2018-0009.

Barrett, Lisa Feldman. *How Emotions are Made*. New York: Houghton Mifflin Harcourt Publishing Company, 2017.

Bell, Lee Anne, and Rosemarie A. Roberts. "The Storytelling Project Model: A Theoretical Framework for Critical Examination of Racism Through the Arts." *Teachers College Record* 112, no. 9 (2010): 2295–319. https://www.researchgate.net/publication/265758206_The_Storytelling_Project_Model_A_Theoretical_Framework_for_Critical_Examination_of_Racism_Through_the_Arts.

Bishop, Kay, and Melanie A. Kimball. "Engaging Students in Storytelling." *Teacher Librarian* 33, no. 4 (2006): 28–31. http://thegatheringteachers.weebly.com/uploads/3/2/1/0/32109417/eci_808_storytelling.pdf.

Brooks, Jacqueline Grennon. "Constructivism." In *Encyclopedia of Cognitive Science*, edited by L. Nadel. New York: Wiley, 2005. https://onlinelibrary.wiley.com/doi/book/10.1002/0470018860.

Chancellor, Reante, and Shari Lee. "Storytelling: Oral History and Building the Library Community." *Storytelling, Self, Society: Storytelling in Libraries* 12, no. 12 (2016): 39–54. https://doi.org/10.13110/storselfsoci.12.1.0039.

Cherry, Jr., Wayne R. "Our Place in the Universe: The Importance of Story and Storytelling in the Classroom." *Knowledge Quest* 46, no. 2 (2017): 50–55.

Cron, Lisa. *Wired for Story: The Writer's Guide to Using Brain Science to Hook Readers from the Very First Sentence*. New York: Ten Speed Press, 2012.

Delgado, Richard. "Storytelling for Oppositionists and Others: A Plea for Narrative." *Michigan Law Review Association* 87, no. 8 (1989): 2411–41. https://doi.org/10.2307/1289308.

Detmering, Robert, and Anna Marie Johnson. "'Research Papers Have Always Seemed Very Daunting': Information Literacy Narratives and the Student Research Experience." *portal: Libraries and the Academy* 12, no. 1 (2012): 5–22. https://doi.org/10.1353/pla.2012.0004.

Edwards, Ashley. "Unsettling the Future by Uncovering the Past: Decolonizing Academic Libraries and Librarianship." *Partnership: The Canadian Journal of Library and Information Practice and Research* 14, no. 1 (2019): 1–11. https://journal.lib.uoguelph.ca/index.php/perj/article/view/5161.

Ewick, Patricia, and Susan S. Silbey. "Subversive Stories and Hegemonic Tales: Toward a Sociology of Narrative." *Law & Society Review* 29, no. 2 (1995): 197–226. https://doi.org/10.1086/378035.

Gottschall, Jonathan. *The Storytelling Animal: How Stories Make Us Human*. New York: Houghton Mifflin Harcourt Publishing Company, 2012.

Hughes-Hassell, Sandra. "Multicultural Young Adult Literature as a Form of County-Storytelling." *The Library Quarterly: Information, Community, Policy* 83, no. 3 (2013): 212–28. https://doi.org/10.1086/670696.

Justice, Daniel Heath. *Why Indigenous Literatures Matter*. Waterloo, Ontario: Wilfrid Laurier University Press, 2018.

Krathwohl, David R., Benjamin S. Bloom, and Bertram B. Masia. *Taxonomy of Educational Objectives, the Classification of Educational Goals. Handbook II: Affective Domain*. New York: David McKay Co, Inc., 1964.

Lamott, Anne. *Bird by Bird*. New York: Anchor Books, 1995.

Lee & Low Books. "Where is the Diversity in Publishing? The 2019 Diversity Baseline Survey Results." *The Open Book Blog* (blog), January 28, 2020. https://blog.leeandlow.com/2020/01/28/2019diversitybaselinesurvey/.

Leeming, David Adams. *Storytelling Encyclopedia, Historical, Cultural, and Multiethnic Approaches to Oral Traditions Around the World*. Phoenix, AZ: The Oryx Press, 1997.

Lipman, Doug. *Improving Your Storytelling: Beyond the Basics for All Who Tell Stories in Work or Play*. Little Rock, AR: August House, 1999.

Lockman, Rachel. "Academic Librarians and Social Justice: A Call to Microactivism." *College and Research Libraries News* 76, no. 4 (2015). https://crln.acrl.org/index.php/crlnews/article/view/9292/10372#b5-0760193.

Loy, David. *The World is Made of Stories*. Boston, MA: Wisdom Publications, 2010.

McDowell, Kate. "Storytelling: Practice and Process as Non-Textual Pedagogy." *Education for Information* 34, no. 1 (2018): 15–19. https://doi.org/10.3233/EFI-189003.

McIntosh, Peggy. "White Privilege: Unpacking the Invisible Knapsack." *Peace and Freedom Magazine* (July/August 1989).
Mooney, William, and David Holt. *The Storyteller's Guide: Storytellers Share Advice for the Classroom, Boardroom, Showroom, Podium, Pulpit, and Center Stage*. Little Rock, AR: August House, 1996.
Morales, Myrna, Em Claire Knowles, and Chris Bourg. "Diversity, Social Justice, and the Future of Libraries." *portal: Libraries and the Academy* 14, no. 3 (2014): 439–51. https://doi.org/10.1353/pla.2014.0017.
National Storytelling Network. "What is Storytelling?" Accessed February 12, 2021. https://storynet.org/what-is-storytelling/.
Palmer, Barbara C., Shelley J. Harshbarger, and Cindy A. Koch. "Storytelling as a Constructivist Model for Developing Language and Literacy." *Journal of Poetry Therapy* 14 (2001): 199–212. https://doi.org/10.1023/A:1017541527998.
Pawley, Christine. "Unequal Legacies: Race and Multiculturalism in the LIS Curriculum." *The Library Quarterly: Information, Community, Policy* 76, no. 2 (2006): 149–68. https://doi.org/10.1086/506955.
Quarry, Justin. "Coming Out as Working Class." *The Chronicle of Higher Education* (October 25, 2018). https://www.chronicle.com/article/coming-out-as-working-class/.
Schank, Roger C. *Tell Me a Story: Narrative and Intelligence*. Evanston, IL: Northwestern University Press, 1990.
Smith, Daniel, Philip Schlaepfer, Katie Major, Mark Dyble, Abigail E. Page, James Thompson, Nikhil Chaudhary, Gul Deniz Salali, Ruth Mace, Leonora Astete, et al. "Cooperation and the Evolution of Hunter-Gatherer Storytelling." *Nature Communications* 8 (2017): 1–9. https://www.nature.com/articles/s41467-017-02036-8.
Solorzano, Daniel G., and Tara J. Yosso. "Critical Race Methodology: Counter-Storytelling as an Analytical Framework for Education Research." *Qualitative Inquiry* 8, no. 1 (2002): 23–44. https://doi.org/10.1177/107780040200800103.
Steslow, Donna M., and Carolyn Gardner. "More Than One Way to Tell a Story: Integrating Storytelling into Your Law Course." *Journal of Legal Studies Education* 28, no. 2 (2011): 249–71. https://doi.org/10.1111/j.1744-1722.2011.01091.x.
Storr, Will. *The Science of Storytelling: Why Stories Make Us Human and How to Tell Them Better*. Read by the author. Audiobook, 7 hr., 3 min. New York: HarperCollins Publishers, 2019.
Strum, Brian W., and Sarah Beth Nelson. "What Can Folktales Teach Us about Higher Education Teaching?" *Storytelling, Self, Society* 13, no. 2 (2017): 170–94. https://digitalcommons.wayne.edu/storytelling/vol13/iss2/3.
Szurmak, Joanna, and Mindy Thuna. "Tell Me a Story: The Use of Narrative as Tool for Instruction." In *Imagine, Innovate, Inspire: The Proceedings of the ACRL 2013 Conference*, edited by D. M. Mueller. American Library Association, 2013. http://www.ala.org/acrl/sites/ala.org.acrl/files/content/conferences/confsandpreconfs/2013/papers/SzurmakThuna_TellMe.pdf.
Terrell, John. "Storytelling and Prehistory." *Archaeological Method and Theory* 2 (1990): 1–29. https://www.jstor.org/stable/20170203.
Vansina, Jan. *Oral Tradition as History*. Madison, WI: University of Wisconsin Press, 1985.
Vossler, Joshua J., and John Watts. "Educational Story as a Tool for Addressing the Framework for Information Literacy for Higher Education." *portal: Libraries and the Academy* 17, no. 3 (2017): 529–42. https://doi.org/10.1353/pla.2017.0033.
Watson, James, and Anne Hill. "Narrative paradigm." *Dictionary of Media and Communication Studies*. 9th ed. New York: Bloomsbury Publishing, 2015.

Woodhouse, Howard. "Storytelling in University Education: Emotion, Teachable Moments, and the Value of Life." *The Journal of Educational Thought* 45, no. 3 (2011): 212–38. https://www.jstor.org/stable/23767205.

Woods, Elin, and Sara Parme. "Fight the Power: Giving Voice to Student Concerns About Textbook Prices." Lecture, SSHELCO Virtual Conference, April 10, 2020.

Chapter 1

A Tale of Five Case Studies:

Reflections on Piloting a Case-Based, Problem-Based Learning Curriculum in English Composition

Katie Strand, Rachel Wishkoski, Alex Sundt, and Deanna Allred

Lively discussions break out in noticeable contrast to the dull, white walls of the windowless library classroom. Four college students immediately dismiss a news article as biased, emotional, and useless. "Remember context and purpose matter," echoes a pointed reminder from the librarian. A case study handout, forgotten and pushed aside since the start of the activity, gets picked up and reread with renewed focus. It explains that Taylor, the subject of the case study, is terrified by a recent article and wants to make their senator aware of their concerns. "Wait…" a member of the group says. "This might actually be useful for Taylor. Let's look at it again."

The source in question for Taylor's group is an editorial in the *Washington Post* arguing for stronger regulation of 3D-printed guns. Taylor's case study, along with four others distributed across several small groups, provides the foundation for today's source evaluation activity. Using these real-world scenarios, students explore complex questions of authority and bias, while also considering the context and purpose of subjects in their case studies. In a reflection assignment a few days later, a student muses, "Monday, the library day, was very helpful in learning how to evaluate sources, which is something I struggle with. I did not realize that so much research needed to be done about research."

When the class reconvenes in the library two weeks later—this time to practice identifying new facets of a research topic and finding sources using library databases—Taylor's group is energetic and engaged. Their exploration takes them down interesting paths, from 3D-printed ammo to the Second Amendment to broader issues with 3D printing technology. When the team shares their brainstorming and receives feedback from another group, it's clear that they're not just invested in Taylor's topic, they've also made a personal connection with their case study and put themselves in Taylor's shoes.

The team has the opportunity to step into Taylor's shoes one last time for a third and final library session. Passionate and eager to find a thoughtful solution to a complex issue, the group dives into synthesizing the sources they've found with additional sources provided by the librarians using a research matrix. The students then transition into writing, picking a main idea and drafting a paragraph weaving together evidence from various sources to support their claim. Bits of conversation rise above the din as each case study team races to write a compelling paragraph: "What argument is going to be the most persuasive?" "This is good, but it could be better with a stronger bit of evidence…." "Well, we can't say that because it would contradict what we just said…." and "We need a conclusion…." After the frenzy of drafting is done, everyone takes a breath before swapping their work for peer review. The students reviewing the paragraph written by Taylor's team are impressed; they cited three sources and addressed a counterargument while making a compelling claim. The student who pushed to include the counterargument smiled and shrugged in a gesture of "Yeah, I did that." As everyone begins trickling out of the room at the end of class, one student comments that he is considering using the topic for his final research paper and admits, half-joking, "That was probably the best paragraph I've ever written!"

Storytelling Goal

Storytelling was used as a method to teach research as real-world problem-solving. Through the use of case studies, storytelling provided lower-stakes scenarios through which students could practice source evaluation, topic development, and synthesis before beginning their own research projects. Building on the narrative foundation of their case studies, students were encouraged to consider different perspectives and enter a creative space as they collaboratively researched a topic and co-created artifacts that reflected their shared journey as researchers.

Audience

Students enrolled in ENGL 2010, a required general education course at Utah State University titled Intermediate Writing: Research Writing in a Persuasive Mode.

Every Utah State University student must pass ENGL 2010 in order to graduate. Seventy to eighty face-to-face sections of the course are offered each semester on the Logan campus, with additional sections offered online and through synchronous videoconferencing. On the Logan campus, ENGL 2010 students are typically first- and second-year students, though students may also be non-traditional or choose to postpone the course for later in their academic careers. As most have not yet declared a major, ENGL 2010 students have varied interests and academic goals.

ENGL 2010 and its prerequisite ENGL 1010 have their own separate objectives and learning outcomes, with the overall goal being that once students have finished the sequence, they will have developed foundational research and writing skills related to rhetorical argumentation. Students are sometimes reluctant to take English 2010, though the writing, rhetorical, and information literacy skills covered in the course are foundational to their work in future courses and necessary for becoming an informed and engaged professional and community member post-graduation. The culmination of ENGL 2010 is a ten- to twelve-page persuasive paper on a topic of each student's choice. Some wish to write about current controversies or hot-button social and political issues, though the most successful papers typically explore topics that are personally meaningful to their authors and applicable to their future goals. In their work, students engage deeply with rhetorical strategies such as ethos, pathos, logos, kairos, audience, purpose, and effective engagement with opposing views.

Delivery

The library's integration with ENGL 2010 is delivered over the course of three library instruction sessions, with lessons that are grounded in active learning principles. Library lessons focus on source evaluation, topic investigation, and synthesis, and are designed to help students research and write a personal research essay (PRE). Originally, case studies were only used for our first lesson on source evaluation. But after observing high engagement from students in response to this approach, we wanted to test the benefits of using case-based, problem-based learning across the full sequence of lessons. We modified and piloted the new lessons with two fifty-minute sections of ENGL 2010 in fall 2019. For the modified lessons, students were grouped together and assigned one of five case studies, which they continued using across each subsequent instruction session.

Table 1.1 Case studies used in our fall 2019 curriculum		
Name	Scenario	Source
Taylor	Using a news source to lobby a senator	Editorial Board. "3-D-printed guns put carnage a click away." *The Washington Post*, July 28, 2018. https://www.washingtonpost.com/opinions/3-d-printed-guns-put-carnage-a-click-away/2018/07/28/3b254a18-91cb-11e8-b769- e3fff17f0689_story.html?arc404=true.
McKenzie	Using a popular source in an English 2010 essay	Haberstroh, Tom. "Who's the NBA's GOAT? Lebron May Have Already Answered the Question." *Bleacher Report*, 31 May 2018. https://bleacherreport.com/articles/2778733whos-the-nbas-goat-lebron-may-have-already-answered-the-question.

Table 1.1 Case studies used in our fall 2019 curriculum

Name	Scenario	Source
Eric	Using an irrelevant scholarly article to petition city council	Morel, Chantel M., et al. "Cost-Effectiveness of Long-Lasting Insecticide-Treated Hammocks in Preventing Malaria in South-Central Vietnam." *PlosONE*, vol. 8, no. 3, March 2013. https://doi.org/10.1371/journal.pone.0058205.
Oliver	Using a satirical website to back a business plan	Maloney, Catherine, et al. "Feline Reactions to Bearded Men." *Improbable Research*. http://www.improbable.com/airchives/classical/cat/cat.html.
Brie	Using a blog for health advice	Sadeghi, Habib. "Could There Possibly Be a Link Between Underwire Bras and Breast Cancer?" *Goop*, 19 December 2017. goop.com/wellness/health/could-there-possibly-be-a-link-between-underwire-bras-and-breast-cancer/. Note: Brie's article is available as a PDF at https://tinyurl.com/engl2010brie because the original was ultimately taken down by Goop.

Lessons began with a brief lecture that introduced a concept or skill, then transitioned into a discussion or free-write activity that helped frame small-group activities. The evaluating sources lesson incorporated a think/pair/share discussion to surface strategies students already leverage to evaluate information. We connected these to an infographic we developed to invite students to consider their prior knowledge and emotion, take an iterative approach to evaluation, and encourage lateral searching. Students used this infographic to evaluate their case study's source in their small groups. The topic investigation lesson asked students to revisit their case study's topic from new angles. They cultivated an inquisitive approach to research through mind mapping, using Academic Search Ultimate to uncover new angles, peer review, and intentional reflection on alternate viewpoints. The final lesson, covering synthesis, required students to read two sources they had found and selected from their research in the previous library visit and then incorporate ideas and evidence from them into a partially completed synthesis matrix. The case study teams then used the matrix to practice writing a paragraph that wove together multiple sources and ideas to make a claim. Peer review and debrief discussion helped students connect these in-class activities to their own processes of organizing research and writing before they were required to create and write from their own matrix for their culminating individual research paper.

Sessions were co-taught by two librarians who shared the roles of lecturing, facilitating discussions and activities, and helping students one-on-one. Because class sessions only lasted fifty minutes, lessons followed a tight schedule, with each portion timed closely to facilitate a smooth transition to each learning objective. Lessons were delivered in one of the library's open-plan instruction labs, which provided a flexible space that was well-suited for large classroom discussions as well as small group activities and individual research.

Theory

Moments like those described in this chapter's opening scenes, where students are meaningfully engaging with research materials and processes, demonstrate the power of case-based, problem-based learning (CBPBL) in library instruction. Case studies offer students narrative spaces in which to practice applying a range of information literacy and critical-thinking skills to a relevant scenario as a team. As Linda Carder, Patricia Willingham, and David Bibb explain, the "tightly focused mini-cases" in a CBPBL approach invite students to connect to "the problems or dilemmas faced by the character(s) in the narrative, calling upon the students' use of information gathering and decision-making skills in identifying key issues and postulating possible solutions."[1] The sequence of lessons in our pilot curriculum used CBPBL to allow students to actively work through the research process within the context of a single case study.

Case-based learning is a more structured form of problem-based learning (PBL).[2] Initially developed in the 1960s as curriculum reform for medical education, PBL has been adapted for many disciplines and instructional contexts, including information literacy instruction.[3] Academic librarians have used this approach in a wide range of teaching scenarios.[4] English composition and technical writing instructors have also adapted PBL in their college and university classrooms.[5] Both librarians and English instructors have experienced positive impacts using PBL and CBPBL approaches to foster student engagement, collaboration, problem-solving strategies, writing skills, and understanding of the "real-world value"[6] of classroom learning.

Our story with CBPBL began in summer 2018 when the three librarians of our team put our heads together to re-think how we were teaching source evaluation to students in ENGL 2010. Drawing from previous uses of CBPBL in library curricula, our new source evaluation lesson was framed around five first-person narratives, presented as research case studies, that described how and why a source was being used. Our fictional researchers were designed to seem like peers, but rather than only reflect academic research contexts, we deliberately modeled our case studies to include real-world problems students might encounter beyond their academic lives. This provided a narrative hook, inviting students to step into the shoes of our characters and adopt a different perspective while they worked in groups to practice critically evaluating a text.

Anecdotally, using case studies seemed to better connect with students' experiences and engage them more deeply in the lesson material. After observing the success of this approach, we recruited an additional team member, an ENGL 2010 lecturer, to tackle a larger-scale project: developing, delivering, and assessing a library curriculum grounded in CBPBL theory. Using our five case studies to frame learning objectives and activities across each library session, we hoped to create a common plotline that would connect lessons on source evaluation, topic development, and information synthesis.

We strategically took a more structured approach to CBPBL than what is typical for traditional problem-based learning. When teaching these lessons, we were faced with the time constraint of three fifty-minute class sessions. We utilized worksheets in each lesson to provide enough structure to keep students synchronously moving through the research process, while still allowing them the freedom to make critical decisions about their case study's research. Although fruitful group discussions and time for unpacking complex concepts were sometimes cut short, this approach allowed us to meet specific information literacy learning outcomes in a limited amount of class time. Details about our assessment methods and results are available in an article published in *Reference Services Review*.[7]

Though the CBPBL approach was not enjoyed by all our learners, some of our students expressed in their own words what we had intended with our pedagogy. One student noted that the case studies offered a lower-stakes opportunity to learn without having to feel added pressure from their own assignment topic: "Learning and using research skills for another person's idea helped me learn how to navigate academic search engines and how to find sources that I desired. The low-stress environment of the library and the help of others made the idea of doing academic research much less intimidating and it actually was a fun experience." Even as some students grew reluctant to continue using the case studies, many still derived value from the lessons. For example, one student commented, "Every time we had [a library session], I was hesitant and wasn't sure what more we could possibly do with the case studies, but I was always pleasantly surprised at how useful they were. I think the best ones were the research and the synthesis day."

Cultural Considerations

Developing our case study personas and topics was a challenge as we reflected on issues of representation and power in the stories we were creating. On the one hand, we wanted our case studies to resonate with and reflect our learners' experiences and the information-seeking problems they might be facing now or could be confronted with in the future. For example, one case study is an ENGL 2010 student writing their persuasive essay, but other topics were deliberately non-academic, such as our case study on healthcare misinformation, signaling the role that evaluation, research, and synthesis can also play in everyday life. However, we also knew it was important to have our case studies provide representation more broadly in the facets of the characters and situations we were creating. Though our student body is not homogenous, the majority of its members identify as white and as part of Utah's predominant religious and political communities. For those students who identify as part of the majority, we wanted the case studies to showcase diversity. For students who do not, we hoped deliberate representations of diversity would signal inclusion in addition to the other inclusive teaching practices we strive for in our work.

As we created our case studies, we considered representation in terms of racial, ethnic, and gender identity, and avoided assigning topics based on any stereotypes about particular identities. We created a non-binary case study (Taylor) with they/them pronouns and used an image from Vice Media's "Gender Spectrum Collection," a collection of stock photos with trans and non-binary models.[8] While perhaps appearing subtle, these choices do matter. In the case of our pilot, they also contributed to one of the course instructor's learning goals: facilitating opportunities for students to think critically about their "cultural eye" and consider cultural and social perspectives different from their own. In a reflection on the first library lesson about evaluating sources, one member of the Brie case study group wrote the following: "I was able to contribute a unique opinion to my group, being the only male. This article didn't register to my mind because I have never worn a bra. Instead of thinking of how this affected me personally, I researched the author of the article to find out his cultural eye."

Reflecting on and observing our teaching provided another lens through which we can improve our lessons. After developing our case studies and activities to accompany them, our pilot project was intentionally designed to provide ample opportunities for peer observation and reflection as well as time for instructor debrief and discussion, making it feel like an immersive, active learning experience for us as teachers. On reflection, we recognize our case studies are not perfect and could be more diverse and more inclusive, both in their depictions of underrepresented groups and in providing research topics that would appeal to different learning styles. Moving forward to make CBPBL better in this respect, it would be helpful to develop a menu of case studies that perhaps students could choose from. Longer scenario stories would also give us more room to tell diverse stories. Though we did involve student employees and interns in some of our case study development, it would be helpful to engage them in the creation of additional cases. Finally, it would be powerful to consider how themes of justice could be embedded in case study narratives and become tools for more meaningful discussion, particularly by opening questions about the politics and power of information.

As Maria Barefoot has demonstrated, PBL can be a successful means of teaching cultural literacy and empathy alongside information literacy.[9]

Practical Examples

TAYLOR

Editorial Board. "3-D-printed guns put carnage a click away." The Washington Post, July 28 2018. https://www.washingtonpost.com/opinions/3-d-printed-guns-put-carnage-a-click-away/2018/07/28/3b254a18-91cb-11e8-b769-e3fff17f0689_story.html?arc404=true.

PURPOSE

I just learned that people can just print their own guns, and there are no regulations on this at all. I'm so charged up I'm emailing my senator immediately to get this under control! I found this article that really shows the danger this could pose to society. Is this a good article to include in my email and spur my senator into action?

MCKENZIE

Haberstroh, Tom. "Who's the NBA's GOAT? Lebron May Have Already Answered the Question." Bleacher Report. 31 May 2018. bleacherreport.com/articles/2778733 whos-the-nbas-goat-lebron-may-have-already-answered-the-question

PURPOSE

I am writing a persuasive research paper for my college English course, and we were told to choose a topic that we feel passionate about. There's nothing I am more passionate about than proving that Lebron James is a better athlete than Michael Jordan. He's just better no matter how you slice it! I found this great article that drives my point home, but I am worried it's not good enough for college level research. Do you think I can use this one or should I dive back into those stuffy scholarly journals?

ERIC

Morel, Chantel M., et al. "Cost-Effectiveness of Long-Lasting Insecticide-Treated Hammocks in Preventing Malaria in South-Central Vietnam." Plos ONE, vol. 8, no. 3, Mar. 2013. doi:10.1371/journal.pone.0058205.

PURPOSE

What is this world coming to? A citywide ban on hammocks in public spaces has been put into effect. As president of my hammocking club, I am devastated as our entire way of life is being ripped away from us! Along with my fellow hammocking enthusiasts, I will be addressing the city council. I found a scientific article that proves that hammocks have health benefits. Is this the article that will make Logan city reverse the ban?

A Tale of Five Case Studies 39

OLIVER

Maloney, Catherine, et al. "Feline Reactions to Bearded Men." Improbable Research, www.improbable.com/airchives/classical/cat/cat.html.

PURPOSE

Hey! I am doing research for a business pitch to potential investors. I am dreaming of opening my own barber shop/cat cafe called Kitty Kuts. I found this fantastic study where researchers analyzed how cats react to bearded individuals to use in my presentation. Is this the article that is going to make my investors purr?

BRIE

Sadeghi, Habib. "Could There Possibly Be a Link Between Underwire Bras and Breast Cancer??" Goop, 19 Dec. 2017.
goop.com/wellness/health/could-there-possibly-be-a-link-between-underwire-bras-and-breast-cancer/.

Read at: tinyurl.com/engl2010brie

PURPOSE

I don't mean to scare you, but yesterday I stumbled upon this terrifying article. It was written by an actual doctor and basically says that bras cause cancer! I have so many girlfriends on social media and you know they just put one of those Victoria Secrets in at the mall. I feel like I have an obligation as a woman to share this with as many people as possible. It could save lives! Should I hit that share button and pass this important health information along?

Endnotes

1. Linda Carder, Patricia Willingham, and David Bibb, "Case-Based, Problem-Based Learning: Information Literacy for the Real World," *Research Strategies* 18, no. 3 (2001): 181.
2. Dawn E. Hackman, Susan K. Cavanaugh, and Annie Nickum, "Librarians as Facilitators in the Active Learning Curriculum," in *The Engaged Health Sciences Library Liaison*, eds. Lindsay Alcock and Kelly Thormodson (Lanham: Rowan & Littlefield, 2019): 71–86.
3. Alexis Smith Macklin, "Integrating Information Literacy Using Problem-Based Learning," *Reference Services Review* 29, no. 4 (2001): 306–14, https://doi.org/10.1108/eum0000000006493; Kate Wenger, "Problem-Based Learning and Information Literacy: A Natural Partnership," *Pennsylvania Libraries: Research & Practice* 2, no. 2 (Fall 2014): 142–54, https://doi.org/10.5195/palrap.2014.61.
4. Alan Carbery, "Introducing Problem-Based Learning into One-Shot Information Literacy Instruction at Waterford Institute of Technology Libraries," *SCONUL Focus* 53 (2011): 30–33; Peg Cook and Mary Barbara Walsh, "Collaboration and Problem-Based Learning: Integrating Information Literacy into a Political Science Course," *Communications in Information Literacy* 6, no. 1 (2012): 59–72, https://doi.org/10.15760/comminfolit.2012.6.1.118; Barbara J. D'Angelo, "Using Source Analysis to Promote Critical Thinking," *Research Strategies* 18, no. 4 (2001): 303–09, https://doi.org/10.1016/s0734-3310(03)00006-5; Anne R. Diekema, Wendy Holliday, and Heather Leary, "Re-Framing Information Literacy: Problem-Based Learning as Informed Learning," *Library & Information Science Research* 33, no. 4 (2011): 261–68, https://doi.org/10.1016/j.lisr.2011.02.002; Kathy Brock Enger et al., "Problem-Based Learning: Evolving Strategies and Conversations for Library Instruction," *Reference Services Review* 30, no. 4 (2002): 355–58, https://doi.org/10.1108/00907320210451367; Anne Glusker, "Motivational Design and Problem-Based Learning May Increase Student Engagement in Information Literacy Instruction Sessions," *Evidence Based Library & Information Practice* 12, no. 4 (2017): 259–61, https://doi.org/10.18438/b8pq1k; Barbara Ferrer Kenney, "Revitalizing the One-Shot Instruction Session Using Problem-Based Learning," *Reference & User Services Quarterly* 47, no. 4 (2008): 386–91, https://doi.org/10.5860/rusq.47n4.386; Alexis Smith Macklin, "A PBL Approach for Teaching Complex Information and Communication Technology (ICT) Skills in Higher Education," *Community & Junior College Libraries* 14, no. 4 (2008): 233–49, https://doi.org/10.1080/02763910802336381; Vivian Milczarski and Amanda Maynard, "Improving Information Literacy Skills for Psychology Majors: The Development of a Case Study Technique," *College & Undergraduate Libraries* 22, no. 1 (2015): 35–44, https://doi.org/10.1080/10691316.2015.1001242; Lindsay Roberts, "Research in the Real World: Improving Adult Learners Web Search and Evaluation Skills through Motivational Design and Problem-Based Learning," *College & Research Libraries* 78, no. 4 (May 2017): 527–51, https://doi.org/10.5860/crl.78.4.527; Andy Spackman and Leticia Camacho, "Rendering Information Literacy Relevant: A Case-Based Pedagogy," *Journal of Academic Librarianship* 35, no. 6 (November 2009): 548–54, https://doi.org/10.1016/j.acalib.2009.08.005.
5. Lisa Beckelhimer et al., "Problem-Based Composition: The Practical Side," *The CEA Forum* 36, no. 1 (Winter/Spring 2007): 1–7; Kelly Diamond, "Problem-Based Learning and Information Literacy: Revising a Technical Writing Class," in *Teaching Information Literacy and Writing Studies: Volume 2, Upper-Level and Graduate Courses*, ed.

Grace Veach (West Lafayette: Purdue University Press, 2019): 157–68; Rita Kumar and Brenda Refaei, "Designing a Problem-Based Learning Intermediate Composition Course," *College Teaching* 61, no. 2 (2013): 67–73, https://doi.org/10.1080/87567555.2012.741079; Paula Rosinski and Tim Peeples, "Forging Rhetorical Subjects: Problem-Based Learning in the Writing Classroom," *Composition Studies* 40, no. 2 (Fall 2012): 9–33.
6. Beckelhimer et al., "Problem-Based Composition," 4.
7. Rachel Wishkoski et al., "Case Studies in The Classroom: Assessing A Pilot Information Literacy Curriculum for English Composition," *Reference Services Review* 49, no. 2 (2020): 176-193, https://doi.org/10.1108/RSR-01-2021-0004.
8. Vice Media Group and Zackary Drucker, "The Gender Spectrum Collection," accessed January 7, 2021, https://genderphotos.vice.com/.
9. Maria R. Barefoot, "Identifying Information Need through Storytelling," *Reference Services Review* 46, no. 2 (2018): 251–63, https://doi.org/10.1108/RSR-02-2018-0009.

Bibliography

Barefoot, Maria R. "Identifying Information Need through Storytelling." *Reference Services Review* 46, no. 2 (2018): 251–63. https://doi.org/10.1108/RSR-02-2018-0009.

Beckelhimer, Lisa, Ronald Hundemer, Judith Sharp, and William Zipfel. "Problem-Based Composition: The Practical Side." *The CEA Forum* 36, no. 1 (Winter/Spring 2007): 1–7.

Carbery, Alan. "Introducing Problem-Based Learning into One-Shot Information Literacy Instruction at Waterford Institute of Technology Libraries." *SCONUL Focus* 53 (2011): 30–33.

Carder, Linda, Patricia Willingham, and David Bibb. "Case-Based, Problem-Based Learning: Information Literacy for the Real World." *Research Strategies* 18, no. 3 (2001): 181–90.

Cook, Peg, and Mary Barbara Walsh. "Collaboration and Problem-Based Learning: Integrating Information Literacy into a Political Science Course." *Communications in Information Literacy* 6, no. 1 (2012): 59–72. https://doi.org/10.15760/comminfolit.2012.6.1.118.

D'Angelo, Barbara J. "Using Source Analysis to Promote Critical Thinking." *Research Strategies* 18, no. 4 (2001): 303–09. https://doi.org/10.1016/s0734-3310(03)00006-5.

Diamond, Kelly. "Problem-Based Learning and Information Literacy: Revising a Technical Writing Class." In *Teaching Information Literacy and Writing Studies: Volume 2, Upper-Level and Graduate Courses*, edited by Grace Veach, 157–68. West Lafayette: Purdue University Press, 2019.

Diekema, Anne R., Wendy Holliday, and Heather Leary. "Re-Framing Information Literacy: Problem-Based Learning as Informed Learning." *Library & Information Science Research* 33, no. 4 (2011): 261–68. https://doi.org/10.1016/j.lisr.2011.02.002.

Enger, Kathy Brock, Stephanie Brenenson, Katy Lenn, Margy MacMillan, Michele F. Meisart, Harry Meserve, and Sandra A. Vella. "Problem-Based Learning: Evolving Strategies and Conversations for Library Instruction." *Reference Services Review* 30, no. 4 (2002): 355–58. https://doi.org/10.1108/00907320210451367.

Glusker, Anne. "Motivational Design and Problem-Based Learning May Increase Student Engagement in Information Literacy Instruction Sessions." *Evidence Based Library & Information Practice* 12, no. 4 (2017): 259–61. https://doi.org/10.18438/b8pq1k.

Hackman, Dawn E., Susan K. Cavanaugh, and Annie Nickum. "Librarians as Facilitators in the Active Learning Curriculum." In *The Engaged Health Sciences Library Liaison*,

edited by Lindsay Alcock and Kelly Thormodson, 71–86. Lanham: Rowan & Littlefield, 2019.
Kenney, Barbara Ferrer. "Revitalizing the One-Shot Instruction Session Using Problem-Based Learning." *Reference & User Services Quarterly* 47, no. 4 (2008): 386–91. https://doi.org/10.5860/rusq.47n4.386.
Kumar, Rita, and Brenda Refaei. "Designing a Problem-Based Learning Intermediate Composition Course." *College Teaching* 61, no. 2 (2013): 67–73. https://doi.org/10.1080/87567555.2012.741079.
Macklin, Alexis Smith. "A PBL Approach for Teaching Complex Information and Communication Technology (ICT) Skills in Higher Education." *Community & Junior College Libraries* 14, no. 4 (2008): 233–49. https://doi.org/10.1080/02763910802336381.
———. "Integrating Information Literacy Using Problem-Based Learning." *Reference Services Review* 29, no. 4 (2001): 306–14. https://doi.org/10.1108/eum0000000006493.
Milczarski, Vivian, and Amanda Maynard. "Improving Information Literacy Skills for Psychology Majors: The Development of a Case Study Technique." *College & Undergraduate Libraries* 22, no. 1 (2015): 35–44. https://doi.org/10.1080/10691316.2015.1001242.
Roberts, Lindsay. "Research in the Real World: Improving Adult Learners Web Search and Evaluation Skills through Motivational Design and Problem-Based Learning." *College & Research Libraries* 78, no. 4 (May 2017): 527–51. https://doi.org/10.5860/crl.78.4.527.
Rosinski, Paula, and Tim Peeples. "Forging Rhetorical Subjects: Problem-Based Learning in the Writing Classroom." *Composition Studies* 40, no. 2 (Fall 2012): 9–33.
Spackman, Andy, and Leticia Camacho. "Rendering Information Literacy Relevant: A Case-Based Pedagogy." *Journal of Academic Librarianship* 35, no. 6 (November 2009): 548–54. https://doi.org/10.1016/j.acalib.2009.08.005.
Vice Media Group and Zackary Drucker. "The Gender Spectrum Collection." Accessed January 7, 2021. https://genderphotos.vice.com/.
Wenger, Kate. "Problem-Based Learning and Information Literacy: A Natural Partnership." *Pennsylvania Libraries: Research & Practice* 2, no. 2 (Fall 2014): 142–54. https://doi.org/10.5195/palrap.2014.61.
Wishkoski, Rachel, Katie Strand, Alex Sundt, Deanna Allred, and Diana Meter. "Case Studies in The Classroom: Assessing A Pilot Information Literacy Curriculum for English Composition." *Reference Services Review* 49, no. 2 (2020): 176–193. https://doi.org/10.1108/RSR-01-2021-0004.

Chapter 2

Shooting for the Stars:

Using a Story Ripped from the Astronomy Headlines with First-Year Students

Kathryn Yelinek

It's a hot afternoon in early September. In the library's computer classroom, about twenty first-year students are wandering in for their university seminar class. This class is a basic introduction to university life, and the students have already sat through informational sessions from the writing center and the career center, so for many, this is just another session of someone trying to cram information into their heads. The class is only a one-credit introductory class, and they all know they don't have much research to do, so why are they even having this introduction to the library? This particular section of university seminar is for undeclared students, so most of them aren't even taking intensive classes for their major yet.

One student in the front of the room has already decided what her major is going to be, but she hasn't had a chance to declare it yet. She knows what she wants to write about for the short assignment that they have to do, but she has never used the university's library before and is feeling apprehensive because it's so much bigger than any library she's ever been in. She nervously lines up pens next to her notebook. In the very back row, tucked into a corner, another student has no idea what he's going to write about, and he doesn't really care. He already has his head down on his desk. A third student has written research papers before in high school, so he's preparing to discreetly zone out of the session. He hides his phone under the desk, thinking no one will notice that he's using it in class.

To start the class and to have the students connect to the sample topic used, the librarian—a lifelong stargazer—often selects topics ripped from the astronomy headlines. In the past, she's used examples such as the solar eclipse of 2017 or New Horizons approaching Pluto. While the basic outline of the story remains the same, she can adjust the details to fit the latest astronomical happening and the time frame involved. This time, in the fall of 2019, she's selected to tell the story of Comet Borisov, which has just been discovered. It's the first definitive interstellar comet ever discovered.

The librarian starts by asking the students to think back a few weeks to where they were on the date the comet was discovered. By coincidence, it was the first Friday of the semester. Can they remember where they were doing on that first Friday? This immediately startles the students into paying attention, and there is some chatter among the students as they reminisce with their friends about what they were doing that day. After all, as freshmen, it was their first week away from home! With the students now hooked, the librarian launches into the rest of the story.

Storytelling Goal

To use science to help students understand that library research topics can relate to them, their lives, and the larger world around them, including possible future events.

Audience

Undergraduates, mostly freshmen, in their first few weeks at college. The story presented here was used in slightly different versions with freshmen declared science majors, undeclared freshman students, and an English 101 class of mixed freshmen and sophomores from varying majors. The story details can be altered depending on the audience and expected science savviness.

Delivery

The story was given as an oral presentation. Depending on the audience, a pen can be used as a prop, but it's not required.

The session starts by having the librarian ask students to remember where they were on the day the comet was discovered. This happened to be during the first week of classes. While many students may revel in being away from home for the first time, other students may experience feelings of homesickness or alienation. So while the aim of having students connect emotionally with this timeframe of the comet's discovery is important for the storytelling, for some students the emotions invoked may not be pleasant.

Students enter college with a wide range of scientific literacy skills. Because of this, the level of detail and explanation should be varied depending on the audience. In addition, it is important to stay informed of the latest information concerning a story that is being ripped from the headlines. Information about a newly discovered comet will change as more observations are collected, so the raconteur should attempt to stay informed of this new information. See the supplemental material for examples of how to change the story depending on the audience and developing scientific knowledge.

Theory

Glonek and King found that college students presented with information in a narrative format recalled more information than students presented with the same information in an expository format. They contributed this greater recall to the constructivist theory of narrative comprehension, which states that human beings constantly make inferences while being exposed to a story, which can in turn lead to deeper meaning-making and greater recall.[1] Similarly, Palmer, Harshbarger, and Koch showed that storytelling was an effective way to increase children's language and literacy skills and that through storytelling, children build on their prior knowledge to give meaning to stories and the information conveyed through them.[2]

Having students think back to a particular time and remembering what they were doing at that time allowed the students, through inference, to put themselves in the place of the amateur astronomer. I specifically chose the story of an amateur astronomer because students are usually amateurs in their chosen fields. They could relate more easily to this character than to a more established scientist. I also made sure to highlight actions the main character took, such as posting online, which students were familiar with. This let the students connect with the main character and become emotionally invested in the outcome of the story.

To draw students in further, I used literary devices such as suspense (hinting that astronomers discovered something unexpected about the comet but not immediately revealing what that meant) and repetition (repeating certain phrases to catch the students' attention). I also engaged the visual as well as audio senses of the students in making use of my arm and a pencil to demonstrate how the telescope was positioned or how a celestial body moved through space. Engaging multiple senses allowed the students to immerse themselves more fully into the story.

Like any good story, there was a problem to overcome, namely figuring out what the newly discovered object was. The answer turned out to be an interstellar comet. However, this story did not tie up neatly with a pat ending. In all versions of the story, the ultimate fate of the comet as it made its closest approach to Earth and the Sun was unknown. Since humans are wired to want to know what happens next, this story made use of the students' innate curiosity to keep them engaged with the story both in class and, hopefully, once they left class. While I was unable to complete any follow-up studies with the students to discover if they did in fact draw on their memory of the session for their own research, I can say that I observed more interaction among the students (chattering and exchanging glances) while they recalled where they had been during their first weekend of classes. This is in stark contrast to the looking out of windows or surreptitiously checking of phones under the computer desks that I sometimes receive while introducing sample topics for library sessions. Anecdotally, this tells me the students were paying attention and engaging with the material, which should translate into better recall. Finally, as an instructor, choosing a topic of personal interest allowed me to engage more deeply with the material, which I hope translated into a more engaging delivery for the students.

Cultural Considerations

Because the story being recounted is factual, it retells actual events. One of the truisms of this story is that astronomy—both amateur and professional—continues to be a male-dominated field. The main character of the story is a male amateur astronomer. If this is a concern for a particular audience, the librarian may choose to balance the session by later introducing other examples of female scientists. Historical examples that could be used include Caroline Herschel, Annie Jump Cannon, or Henrietta Leavitt. More recent examples might include Vera Rubin, Katherine Johnson, Carolyn S. Shoemaker, or Katie Bouman.

Practical Example

Here's the story as originally told to a group of undeclared freshmen early in September. [Note: see supplement for examples of how to alter the paragraphs with asterisks for different audiences]

> I'm going to use a sample search for this session. Before I do that search, I want to tell you a story to explain why I picked this search.
>
> Think back to what you were doing on the night of August 30 [2019]. Can you remember what you were doing then? It was the first Friday of the semester. Can you think back to what you were doing then?
>
> [Pause to allow students to remember.]
>
> Well, while you were doing that, halfway around the world in Ukraine, an amateur astronomer was using his telescope to look

at the night sky. He was using his own homemade telescope, which means he was a very good amateur astronomer. I enjoy my fair share of stargazing, but I don't make my own telescopes. So, he's really into it.

This homemade telescope was pretty big for an amateur, but it was still smaller than the huge telescopes professional astronomers use. This means it could tip over far enough to scan the horizon. [It can be helpful here to use your arm to imitate a telescope leaning over far enough to scan the horizon.] And there, along the horizon, the amateur astronomer saw a fuzzy dot. It looked like a comet, but this astronomer knew—because he knew the locations of visible known comets—that there wasn't supposed to be a comet there.

So he did what a good amateur astronomer would do, and he posted online about his discovery, asking if anyone else knew about this fuzzy dot. And no one else did. So good for him, he'd discovered a new comet, quite an achievement for an amateur astronomer.*

Now that astronomers knew about this new comet, they started to observe it, and soon they discovered something unexpected about it. They discovered that it is not gravitationally bound to the Sun. This means it doesn't orbit the Sun like all of the other planets, comets, and such in the solar system. It came from outside the solar system, from outer space. It is an interstellar comet.**

It's the first interstellar comet that's ever been discovered. It will make its closest approach to the Sun and to Earth in December. So while you are studying for finals, keep a watch for news stories about this new interstellar comet. Comets can be atrociously unpredictable when they come close to the Sun, so who knows what it will do. Will it become visible from Earth? Will it break apart? I'm eagerly waiting to find out.***

So, that is my sample topic for class today. We'll be researching comets so you can have a little bit of understanding in case you hear more about this new one later in the semester.****

Supplement

Sample suggestions for altering the story:
   * When working with declared science majors, I liked to emphasize the work that even amateur scientists can do, to encourage their interest in making discoveries still before they had become professionals:

> So he did what a good amateur astronomer would do, and he posted online about his discovery, asking if anyone else knew about this fuzzy dot. And no one else did. So good for him, he'd discovered a new comet, quite an achievement for an amateur astronomer. **It was actually not the first comet he ever discovered. He's discovered several other comets, which shows how good a comet hunter he is.**

   ** When working with declared science majors, I did my best not to talk down to them or define scientific principles they should understand:

> Now that astronomers knew about this new comet, they started to observe it, and soon they discovered something unexpected about it. **They discovered that it is not gravitationally bound to the Sun. It came from outside the solar system.** It is an interstellar comet.

   *** When working with declared since majors, I made references to additional scientific stories they might have heard about in order to spark their interest; later into the fall semester, it became apparent from updated research that the comet would not be visible to the naked eye from Earth:

> It's the first interstellar comet that's ever been discovered. **And it's only the second interstellar object ever discovered. Maybe**

some of you heard about the first one, 'Oumuamua, which was discovered in 2017. If you don't recognize the name, you might have heard on the news that some scientists thought they had discovered a possible alien spacecraft. They thought that because 'Oumuamua doesn't act like a comet or an asteroid or anything else. It seems to be long and skinny like a pen and tumbling through space end over end. [Here is where it can be helpful to use a pen to show an object tumbling end over end through space.] Anyway, this new comet that was discovered definitely is a comet.** It will make its closest approach to the Sun and to Earth in December. So while you are studying for finals, keep a watch for news stories about this new interstellar comet. **While it's unlikely that we'll be able to see the comet from Earth, comets can be atrociously unpredictable when they come close to the Sun, so keep an eye out for late-breaking news stories.**

**** When working with declared science majors, I wanted to mention very briefly that scientific literature can take time to be published and to alert them that more research on the new comet would be forthcoming. This would allow them to consider using the comet as a topic for future research:

> **So, that is my sample topic for class today. There's not a lot of published research yet on the newly discovered comet— scientific research takes time to publish. Instead, we'll be researching comets in general so you can have a little bit of understanding in case you hear more about this new one later in the semester. But if you're looking for a paper topic next semester or in the years to come, the interstellar comet will be a good one to do, because there will be a bucketload of research published on it in the near future.**

Endnotes
1. Katie L. Glonek and Paul E. King, "Listening to Narratives: An Experimental Examination of Storytelling in the Classroom," *The International Journal of Listening* 28 (2014): 38–39.

2. Barbara C. Palmer, Shelley J. Harshbarger, and Cindy A. Koch. "Storytelling as a Constructivist Model for Developing Language and Literacy," *Journal of Poetry Therapy* 14, no. 4 (2001): 209–10.

Bibliography

Glonek, Katie L., and Paul E. King. "Listening to Narratives: An Experimental Examination of Storytelling in the Classroom." *The International Journal of Listening* 28 (2014): 32–46.

Palmer, Barbara C., Shelley J. Harshbarger, and Cindy A. Koch. "Storytelling as a Constructivist Model for Developing Language and Literacy." *Journal of Poetry Therapy* 14, no. 4 (2001): 199–12.

Chapter 3

Encouraging Connections:

Using Personal Storytelling in the Information Literacy Classroom

Allyson Wind and Megan Smith

Imagine being a first-year student at a university. You may have just graduated high school or maybe transferred in from a community college or other institution. You are signed up for a college-level math class. You are eager to learn. You are paying a decent amount of money to get this education and expect a lot from your professor and your college experience in general. You walk into class, have a seat, and fifteen minutes into the lesson, your professor gets distracted and starts telling a tale.

The professor regales you with stories of their time spent working a side gig as a clown. Then to your horror, they leap onto the top of the desk, pull out an air pump and make balloon animals for the rest of your class. For students in your class who don't care as much about doing well in college, this is a perfectly acceptable form of storytelling. The class now knows that mentioning clowns could get the professor off track enough to forget all about math. For you, this is an entire day of valuable learning time lost. At a time when students are choosy about how their education dollars are being spent, this type of storytelling should be avoided in the classroom.

Your next class, however, includes storytelling that is extremely beneficial for you—your University Studies or First-Year Experience Class (FYE). The First-Year Experience's goal is to turn individuals into successful college students and ultimately a college graduate/lifelong learner. Guest speakers from across campus are required to visit the class once during the semester, including the librarians. During the library information session, the librarian teaching your class gets creative with their storytelling. The FYE library sessions start with a fifteen-minute tour of the Kemp Library building. After the tour, the class makes its way to the first-floor computer lab where the librarian teaches about how to navigate the library website and how to search for items in the library catalog and databases.

On the ground floor of the library, toward the tail end of the tour, the tour stops at a memorable place—directly in front of a life-size statue of a cow. The cow is covered in a Mod Podged hodge-podge of images of stamps and was created about a decade ago for each campus in the university system. At this point, the librarian says that we can finally discuss the "elephant in the room," i.e., the cow! The cow is often mentioned as a landmark for scavenger hunts they may be a part of as well as using it to make the tour more interesting. Little do the students know, this part of the tour is a three-part activity: a way to activate their prior knowledge, break the ice, and transition somewhat seamlessly to our next step in the library information session.

Kemp librarians ask the students if they can tell if the cow is male or female and why. This is always a funny activity to do because the cow statue has both horns and an udder, which throws students off, especially those who come from big cities like New York and Philadelphia. Some students say that the cow is a female because it has eyelashes while others say it's a male because of the horns. The librarian then reveals the answer: the cow is female because she has an udder. The librarian mentions that knowing whether a cow is male or female is an important skill to have as a farmer because you do not want to mistake the cows for the bulls in the pasture if you are asked to bring them in for milking. Some students are unaware that some breeds of cows have horns, whether they are male or female. Some horns are removed while others are left on. Horns are not a good way to determine if a cow is male or female. Same with the eyelashes. Both male and female cows (and humans) have eyelashes, so again, not a good way to determine the sex of an animal.

After this activity, the ice has been broken. The entire group is laughing and ready to make our way upstairs to the computer lab. The librarians let students know that we will use the cow as an example for searching the databases because there is a surprising amount of information on cows, from peer-reviewed articles to children's books. This style of storytelling is much more effective than the first example. The student feels energized about attending this class because their teacher is engaged with them and tells a story that directly relates to what they will be learning in the rest of the session. They may not remember everything talked about in class, but they will remember how welcome they felt, that the librarian made them laugh, and will hopefully consider coming to the library for help in the future.

Storytelling Goal

Librarians do not get to spend time with students over the entire semester like their regular professors, so the goal of using storytelling skills is to help build positive, interpersonal relationships with the students in a very short time.

Each fall semester at East Stroudsburg University, all students who are enrolled in the First-Year Experience (FYE) course make their way to Kemp Library to attend an information literacy session taught by one of our faculty librarians. In our one-shot sessions, we strive to activate students' prior knowledge and figure out where they are in the Zone of Proximal Development (see the Theory section of this chapter) so we can adjust our instruction accordingly. As such, no two sessions are ever identical as the content is slightly tailored to each group. The ability to tailor content on the fly is a skill that should be developed and encouraged.

Faculty librarians teach about 150 of these one-shot sessions each fall semester. When one thinks of storytelling, it is easy to envision taking a long time to tell a very detailed story, but due to our time restrictions, we need to make our stories brief and impactful for our students. We only see students one time for forty-five minutes to one hour during a class period per semester. We emphasize to the reader that we do not expect students to retain everything we say during each session, but we want them to leave with the knowledge of where to go for help when they need it and, most importantly, that asking for help is encouraged.

Teaching information literacy skills using the one-shot model can feel impersonal and alienating to students. In order to create a sense of community during this short period, faculty librarians use personal stories to build relationships and add meaning to the topics being discussed. Library faculty act as a bridge between what classroom faculty are teaching and students' prior knowledge and experience. It's important to have a strong link between the stories being told and the material being taught to reassure students that their success is your first priority.

Audience

The primary group that we are addressing with this story is the FYE students we see at the beginning of each academic year. These can be true freshmen, students who have just graduated from high school over the summer, and they could also include transfer students from community colleges or other universities.

Delivery

We use stories in the tour and in the classroom setting. Each librarian has developed their own unique way of storytelling. For example, two librarians say that talking about dietary preferences is an easy way to connect topics that students are interested in; everyone loves to eat! Another librarian uses pop culture references, like discussing favorite superheroes to help highlight the content of our online resources and reinforce the research skills being taught. Personal anecdotes can also be shared with students to connect with them on a more intimate level. Other librarians talk about their own study habits when they were in college, while yet another discusses their career choice to become a librarian after years of teaching elementary school, and other miscellaneous topics that arise based on the circumstances of the particular class session.

In order to replicate this type of storytelling in the classroom, you really can be as creative as possible, and you don't really need any special materials other than your own imagination, an interesting object in the library (like a cow statue!), or perhaps knowledge of what other professors are teaching in the classes your students are taking. Do some brainstorming. Brainstorm about how things you like or that object in the library may tie into what your lesson goal is. Some stories may work better for one part of the class, while others may be better for the tour. The cow, for example, works well for both. It works well for multiple audiences as well, so that story continues to be told. If the topic becomes dry or students stop showing reactions or interest in your story, you can tap into the student's interests to refresh the tales. This works well to reach your ultimate storytelling goal of demonstrating to students that you empathize with them and want them to stick with college and graduate.

Theory

In this age where students are hyper-aware of the value of an education, being able to tell stories that are relevant to the topic being taught is a great way to build positive relationships with your students, activate their prior knowledge, and figure out where they are in Vygotsky's Zone of Proximal Development so you can adjust and scaffold your instruction accordingly and help guide them to become successful researchers.

Certain groups of students, such as ones in the honors section of FYE, may be higher in their abilities to do research, so you can start a little further into the research process than other sections. Many students could have arrived at college with little to no research skills. Some come from high schools with no school librarians, or they may not have a computer or internet access at home.

When we discuss the Zone of Proximal Development here in this chapter, we as librarians are guiding students from where they are to where they should be as information-literate citizens and lifelong learners. Librarians are the experts, and we have the ability to decide how to tailor our stories and assignments to get them to where they need to be.

Cultural Considerations

The cow example from above may be lost on some underrepresented groups served by our university, such as those who are from urban areas. In this case, you could do some brainstorming and tell a story about what everyone has in common: personal dietary preferences.

Librarians like to pepper in a story in our FYE library sessions about how certain professors who teach entry-level English composition will want them to find information on a food-related topic. Even with the cow example, librarians can incorporate stories about our personal dietary choices and discuss drinking milk and eating meat. One librarian likes to talk about the health risks of drinking raw milk because of a personal experience of getting sick. Another librarian will talk about how they are vegan and where to locate government information about the health benefits of veganism. A third librarian uses food deserts as she can tie in several types of real-world concerns to the topic as well as different resource types. These discussions lead to showing students how to locate very relevant library resources based on their topic of choice. You can see a spark in the students' eyes when they realize the library has just what they need for multiple class assignments.

In addition to the personal stories about dietary preferences, all librarians like to talk about our own experiences doing research. Many of our undergraduates who take the entry-level English composition course mentioned in the previous paragraph take a professor who requires them to complete an annotated bibliography. This course is the first time most students have seen one, so we make sure to deconstruct the concept and explain what it is and why it is helpful. Librarians demonstrate several different ways of doing an annotated bibliography since the most effective method varies based on the individual and the assignment. This variation in technique was cleared with the English professor before being shared with the class.

Although at first there was concern that multiple types of annotated bibliographies would be overwhelming or concerning, we found that students actually appreciated the diversity of options and were able to better grasp the concept by having several examples. We also shared a librarian's annotated bibliography that they completed for a paper they wrote as well as some samples of different annotation types to show students how they would/could look. This was used to then show students how creating an annotated bibliography helps write the actual paper. To continue the story after class, students are encouraged to check out our English LibGuide[1] and select the tab for "Annotated Bibliography" to learn more about how we teach annotated bibliographies.

Practical Example

Librarian: Ok class. We've reached the end of our tour here at Kemp Library. I like to stop the tour here because I realized that my tour had been getting a little boring and stopping here makes it a little more interesting. I've learned that most libraries have at least one interesting object in them, and this is ours! This is our cow! Sometimes you'll hear about the cow on a scavenger hunt you may have to take with one of your English classes. It's a pretty popular landmark in the library. Plus, when we go up to the computer lab next, you'll see that there are a lot of things in our catalog and databases about cows.

Both of my parents grew up on dairy farms, so I know a few things about cows. I often hear students debating on whether this cow is male or female so I thought it would be fun to ask tour groups that question from now on.

So …take a look at this cow statue. Can you tell me why it is male or female and why you think that?

Student 1: It's a male!

Librarian: OK, you think it's a male. Why?

Student 1: Because it has horns.

Student 2: I think it's a girl cow because it has eyelashes.

Librarian: That's a good guess! Anyone else? (Waits a couple of seconds.) Let me give you the answer! It's a female because of …THE UDDER! Only female cows have an udder.

Student 1: But what about the horns? I thought bulls had horns.

Librarian: Some breeds of cows have horns. Sometimes they are left on and other times they are removed, but that doesn't hurt them. A bull is a male animal.

Student 3: Wait? Only female cows have an udder?

Librarian: Yes, only female cows have an udder. They also don't give milk all the time. They only give milk once they have a calf.

Student 4: Wow, I didn't know any of this!

Librarian: Well, now you know! When you go out into your career, you'll all have skills that are essential to the job. It's a very important skill to be able to tell whether your bovine is male or female if you're a dairy farmer. You definitely do not want to try and milk a bull!

(At this point everyone is laughing!)

Librarian: This is why I like to end my tour here! You know a little bit more about the library and now you know how to tell whether any cows you meet are male or female. I also like to talk about the cow because I will use "cows" as an example for the next part of our class. We'll be going back up to the main floor computer lab where I'll show you how to navigate the library website.

Endnotes

1. Megan Smith and Elizabeth Scott, "English: Home," English LibGuide, East Stroudsburg University, May 1, 2018, https://esu.libguides.com/c.php?g=832537&p=5943875.

Bibliography

Smith, Megan, and Elizabeth Scott. "English: Home." English LibGuide. East Stroudsburg University, May 1, 2018. https://esu.libguides.com/c.php?g=832537&p=5943875.

Chapter 4

The Moral of the Story Is...
Appealing to Student Values in the Classroom

Gerald R. Natal

It is the start of another one-shot information library session. Like so many others before this one, it is a classroom populated with aspiring nurses, social workers, occupational therapists, and other students from a variety of programs in health sciences and human services. As the students file in, I say hello to each one and personally hand them the day's session outline in an attempt to establish myself as approachable. I observe their actions, hoping to get some idea of the general character of the class as a whole. Many thoughts race through my mind: What sort of day are they having? Will the time of day affect their attention span? Will they be talkative and participatory, reticent, perhaps even disrespectful? How many of them previously had library instruction, and what content was covered? Reading the students is not an easy task, as nearly everyone walks in, sits down in the spot formerly selected as personal territory, and immediately begins checking and sending text messages. I detect no buzz about the room, no sense of excitement; the students received forewarning—today they are having another guest lecturer, this time from the library. This is a room full of students expecting me to

63

demonstrate how to use databases and find articles to complete the next assignment …and little else. I imagine the trajectory for those seated before me, thumbs wildly tapping away, is to find the perfect articles, get an "A" on the paper, ace the class, graduate, and get a well-paying job. They expect a routine and boring presentation on a dry topic. Time seems to slow down as I make small talk with the instructor until at last the clock mercifully signals it is time to start class. The instructor begins, "We have a special guest from the library today—medical librarian Gerald Natal." The title is not exactly accurate, but it is a perfect lead-in to the next sentence: "He's a great resource! Let me tell you about the time a medical librarian saved the life of an entire family who nearly died from food poisoning.…"

Storytelling Goal

In a study to determine students' views on a liberal arts education, the main reasons given for acquiring a college education were job attainment and career advancement, as opposed to gaining the "knowledge, skills, and capacities they actually will need in their working lives."[1] It is therefore not surprising that students (particularly at the undergraduate level) might not think beyond the assignment at hand and fail to see the full value of the library session. I feel it necessary to impart that what I am teaching transcends the agenda to graduate and get a job; these skills are critical for making informed decisions that affect individuals' lives. People will come to them for their expertise for the purposes of healing and improving their quality of life. Consequently, my goal is to convince the students to imagine themselves as professionals applying the days' lesson outside the classroom and consider the outcome of actions taken (or not taken). I make an appeal to the students' sense of duty and the value they personally place on quality health care.

Simply directly stating the importance of knowing how to "do research" is often not persuasive enough; what is required is a change in attitude—a shift in perception, which I hope to accomplish through storytelling (a term I will use throughout to refer to narrative discourse in general, covering analogy, anecdote, metaphor, and narrative). I instinctively follow Garmston's advice to reflect on the intentions of a group before attempting to influence attitudes.[2] This means considering such factors as class composition, motivation, goals, and reasons why the class might be resistant to learning. In support of my overall goal to persuade, I considered several practical objectives from among those suggested by McNett.[3] I chose to *do something unexpected* to *capture the students' attention, personalize* myself (while at the same time establishing myself as an authority) and provide real-world examples (*personalize the content*).

With these goals and objectives in mind, I tell a personal story of my interactions with a physician to illustrate what might happen when a practitioner makes an uninformed decision. I follow this up with a counter-example of a success story of physicians asking for my assistance finding articles to inform their actions during an emergency. One particular faculty member for whom I guest lecture in several classes tells her own story about the heroics of a hospital librarian "before the internet," which lends further credence to my stories and myself as the guest lecturer. My hope is that the students will at least know that I am passionate about what I am about to teach them and that it is not a waste of their time or mine. I wish to convey that as an invited guest speaker, I am more than just "the librarian" but instead an expert not unlike the other "real world" guests invited to speak to them throughout the semester. The immediate goal is for the library instruction that follows to take on new meaning and for the students to be more receptive to learning. Ultimately, I hope to persuade the students that they will be better at their chosen profession for having sat through my information literacy session.

Audience

While I use stories to teach in a variety of situations, the scenarios presented here have to do with undergraduate students in health and human service programs. This includes social work, physical therapy, occupational therapy, speech language pathology, school counseling, criminal justice, exercise science, recreation therapy, respiratory care, and other areas of health education. In addition to the traditional groups of students, I visit a small cohort of high school students taking college-level courses. As the liaison librarian, I visit all of these students (excepting high school) in their required orientation courses. I map my non-orientation instruction sessions to courses with a research component to minimize redundancy; I find it imperative to address the possibility that some students will see the liaison library multiple times. These situations could require flexibility in my use of stories.

Delivery

Oral storytelling takes place under two separate conditions. In the first situation, one particular instructor invites me to all of her classes (multiple sections of three courses). In these cases, she will introduce me with her own story and then I will launch into mine. For all other classes, I will tell one or both of my stories as time and circumstances dictate. Sessions are normally eighty minutes, so there is generally enough time to deliver the stories without compromising the instruction content.

Theory

The use of stories as tools for teaching in a variety of disciplines, settings, and methods in higher education and library science is well established.[4] When used specifically for the purpose of persuasion, storytelling is an effective means for influencing attitudes and behaviors.[5] The use of the narrative as persuasion within storytelling creates conditions whereby students, once immersed in a story, are "transported" into another state of consciousness; students are more receptive to messages and having their perceptions altered in this state, rather than through a more direct delivery.[6] Persuasion is also more apt to occur by arousing emotions, so tapping into students' existing emotions and experiences is essentially the key to enriching their learning experience.[7] The belief that emotional factors are just as important as cognitive factors in teaching indicates that the affective domain is deserving of more attention in the classroom.[8] The ACRL *Framework* supports this notion by embracing the dispositional aspects of information literacy instruction—the "affective, attitudinal, or valuing" dimensions.[9]

Narrative theory seeks to explain this relationship between brain function, narrative, and emotion by suggesting that the human brain actually works by composing stories in a narrative format.[10] During this process, the brain attempts to resolve new information with existing information; this leads to changes in established ways of thinking, which is, in effect, an *emotional experience*.[11] As screenwriter and educator Robert McKee expressed it, stories "fulfill a profound human need to grasp the patterns of living—not merely as an intellectual exercise, but within a very personal, emotional experience."[12] This sentiment points to another important aspect of brain function—the way in which it seeks to resolve new information with existing information through pattern recognition. Established patterns, once applied to new situations, become the basis for new "explanations."[13] Patterns are thus familiar to listeners of stories, which contain the common themes of life's experiences. Within these themes are variations on the narrative pattern that concern goals, obstacles, and the corresponding emotional responses.[14] The ability of the human mind to recognize these macro-narratives—stories that are culturally commonplace and generally recognizable—enables learning.[15]

This general pattern of goal achievement is echoed in the endless stories throughout history in folk tales and myths of the archetypal hero, who undertakes some adventure, encounters obstacles while attempting to achieve a goal, and returns triumphant and transformed (Campbell, 1949).[16] In the story examples used in this writing, the ageless pattern plays out with the librarian in the role of the hero with challenges to overcome, who must seek out the critical information necessary to "save the day." Two of these cases involve patients in life-threatening situations; the third is a more personal story in which the librarian becomes the patient. These scenarios present an opportunity for the creation of an emotional nexus between the storyteller and audience—the students have the chance to relate more personally to the storyteller while approaching the narrative from their own perspective. They may even envision themselves in the hero role and be subtly persuaded to adjust their own attitudes concerning the purpose of the library instruction.

Cultural Considerations

Street referred to literacy as *ideological* and to literacies as social capital used to navigate within communities.[17] In Street's critical view, the teaching of literacy considers culture, student viewpoints, and power relationships between teacher and pupil; within this model, students have the freedom to define their own worldviews. This process of worldmaking is the foremost feature of stories.[18] During the course of storytelling, students have the opportunity to interpret the narrative through the lens of their divergent backgrounds—not as passive listeners, but as co-creators of the storyworld.[19] Such active participation through worldbuilding serves to redefine the power situation in the classroom; the instructor does not simply dictate information, as described in Freire's "banking" model of education in the influential *Pedagogy of the Oppressed*.[20] By imagining themselves within the storyworld of the practitioners, students have occasion to rethink current assumptions and come away transformed through reflective learning. To ensure students' active participation, it is important to be aware that the use of unfamiliar references has the potential to lead to disengagement from the story.[21] This point strengthens the argument for the use of universal themes.[22]

Practical Example
Scenario 1

Surgeons are presented with a dire situation—an entire family critically ill from consuming poison mushrooms. A librarian who peruses medical journals for staff physicians recalls an article concerning the use of dialysis to remove blood toxins and suggests it as a possible solution. The procedure is a life-saving success.

> Course instructor: "We have a special guest from the library today—medical librarian Gerald Natal. He's a great resource! Let me tell you about the time a medical librarian saved the life of an entire family who nearly died from food poisoning! Today, everyone is used to finding the articles they need online. But back in the 'old days' you had to find articles in print copies. At the hospital where I was employed as a social worker, the librarian would scan through the journals' contents and forward copies of articles to the physicians. One day, a family was brought into the hospital with a serious case of food poisoning they had gotten from eating bad mushrooms on a pizza. It so happens the librarian had read of a procedure in one of the medical journals

where blood was cleansed of deadly toxins using dialysis. The librarian suggested the procedure to the attending physicians, who went on to use it to save the life of the family! Now Gerald has a story to tell you—one of my favorite stories."

Scenario 2

Surgeons in a dire situation (a postoperative patient experiencing excessive edema) consult a librarian, who contributes to a successful procedure by supplying the necessary literature on the medical use of leeches.

> Librarian: [Librarian greets the students, introduces self, and asks how many students have had library instruction.] "I was working my designated reference shift one day when I received a phone call from a physician. He had an urgency in his voice—I could hear several voices having a discussion in the background. The doctor explained that they had just performed surgery on an individual who had an ear severed in a motorcycle accident. They were able to attach the ear, but there was a problem—fluid was rapidly building up in the surgical area and causing complications. The physicians were desperately trying to come up with a solution—one of them suggested leeches! Using leeches to "bleed" patients is an old technique, but who'd have thought about leeches in the era of modern medicine! The thing was that none of the doctors knew anything about leeches, and so they called the library. Knowing that the patient was somewhere lying on a table bleeding, I told them I would find them some information and send it immediately. I was able to find seven relevant articles. Later, I received a phone call from the doctor, who told me they were able to locate leeches at the hospital pharmacy! The procedure had been a success, and he thanked me for my part in finding the articles."

Scenario 3

The librarian tells a story of using their research skills to find information on a drug assigned for a personal condition. The librarian discovers the drug is no longer on the market due to adverse reactions in patients. The librarian informs the physician and avoids possible harm to self.

> Librarian: "Let me tell you a more personal story. At one time, I needed treatment for severe allergies and was prescribed medication. Being the librarian that I am, I just had to look up the medication to find out what I was taking. Well, I discovered that the medication had been pulled from the market due to adverse reactions! I immediately called my doctor to ask him if he was aware of the status of the drug he had prescribed and, of course, he was not. I think this story and the others demonstrate the importance of being able to find information to make informed decisions. People will rely on your good judgment to make decisions that will affect their lives, and keeping up with the information in your chosen fields is extremely important. The things you learn in class today go beyond getting an 'A' on your paper—what you learn may improve the quality of someone's life or perhaps even save lives...."

Endnotes

1. Debra Humphries and Abigail Davenport, "What Really Matters in College: How Students View and Value Liberal Education: Liberal Education & America's Promise," *Liberal Education* 91, no. 3 (2005): 38.
2. Robert J. Garmston, *The Astonishing Power of Storytelling* (Thousand Oaks, CA: Corwin, 2018), 96–98.
3. Gabriel McNett, "Using Stories to Facilitate Learning," *College Teaching* 64, no. 4 (2016): 190.
4. McNett, "Using Stories to Facilitate Learning," 184; Joshua J. Vossler and John Watts, "Educational Story as a Tool for Addressing the Framework for Information Literacy for Higher Education," *portal: Libraries and the Academy* 17, no. 3 (2017): 534.
5. M. C. Green and T. C. Brock, "In the Mind's Eye. Transportation-Imagery Model of Narrative Persuasion," in *Narrative Impact. Social and Cognitive Foundations*, ed. M. C. Green, J. J. Strange, and T. C. Brock (Mahwah, NJ: Erlbaum, 2002); Matthew W. Kreuter et al., "Narrative Communication in Cancer Prevention and Control: A Framework to Guide Research and Application," *Annals of Behavioral Medicine* 33, no. 3 (September 2007); M. D. Slater, "Entertainment Education and the Persuasive Impact

of Narratives," in *Narrative Impact: Social and Cognitive Foundations*, ed. M. C. Green, J. J. Strange, and T. C. Brock (Mahwah, NJ: Lawrence Erlbaum Associates, 2002).
6. M. C. Green and T. C. Brock, "The Role of Transportation in the Persuasiveness of Public Narratives," *Journal of Personality and Social Psychology* 79, no. 5 (November 2000): 719.
7. M. H. Immordino-Yang and A. Damasio, "We Feel, Therefore We Learn: The Relevance of Affective and Social Neuroscience to Education," *Mind, Brain, and Education* 1, no. 1 (2007): 9.
8. Vossler and Watts, "Educational Story as a Tool," 531.
9. American Library Association, *Framework for Information Literacy for Higher Education*, http://www.ala.org/acrl/standards/ilframework.
10. Jonathan Gottschall, *The Storytelling Animal: How Stories Make Us Human* (Boston: Mariner Books, 2013), 5; Garmston, *The Astonishing Power of Storytelling*, 19–20; Steven Pinker, *How the Mind Works* (New York: W. W. Norton, 2009), 539; Theodore R. Sarbin, ed. *Narrative Psychology: The Storied Nature of Human Conduct* (New York: Praeger, 1986), 8.
11. Nancy Stein, Bennett Leventhal, and Tom Trabasso, eds., *Psychological and Biological Approaches to Emotion* (Hilllsdale, NJ: Laurence, Erlbaum Associates, 1990), 46.
12. Robert McKee, *Story: Style, Structure, Substance, and the Principles of Screenwriting* (New York: Harper Collins, 1997), 12.
13. Roger C. Schank, *Explanation Patterns: Understanding Mechanically and Creatively* (Hillsdale, NJ: L. Erlbaum Associates, 1986), 109–13.
14. Arthur C. Graesser, Murray Singer, and Tom Trabasso, "Constructing Inferences During Narrative Text Comprehension," *Psychological Review* 101, no. 3 (1994): 372.
15. Jaclyn R. Devine, Todd Quinn, and Paulita Aguilar, "Teaching and Transforming through Stories: An Exploration of Macro- and Micro-Narratives as Teaching Tools," *The Reference Librarian* 55, no. 4 (2014): 274.
16. Joseph Campbell, *The Hero with a Thousand Faces*, 2nd ed. (Princeton, NJ: Princeton University Press, 1968).
17. Brian V. Street, "What's 'New' in the New Literacy Studies: Current Approaches to Literacy in Theory and Practice," *Current Issues in Comparative Education* 5, no. 2 (1993): 77–78.
18. David Herman et al., *Narrative Theory: Core Concepts & Critical Debates* (Columbus: The Ohio State University Press, 2012), 14.
19. Herman et al., *Narrative Theory*, 15.
20. Paulo Freire, *Pedagogy of the Oppressed* (New York: Continuum, 1970), 61.
21. Mindy Thuna and Joanna Szurmak, "Telling Their Stories: A Study of Librarians' Use of Narrative in Instruction," *Journal of Academic Librarianship* 45, no. 5 (2019): 9.
22. Devine, Quinn, and Aguilar, "Teaching and Transforming through Stories," 281.

Bibliography

American Library Association. *Framework for Information Literacy for Higher Education*. http://www.ala.org/acrl/standards/ilframework.

Campbell, Joseph. *The Hero with a Thousand Faces*. 2nd ed. Princeton, NJ: Princeton University Press, 1968.

Devine, Jaclyn R., Todd Quinn, and Paulita Aguilar. "Teaching and Transforming through Stories: An Exploration of Macro- and Micro-Narratives as Teaching Tools." *The Reference Librarian* 55, no. 4 (2014): 273–88.

Freire, Paulo. *Pedagogy of the Oppressed.* New York: Continuum, 1970.
Garmston, Robert J. *The Astonishing Power of Storytelling.* Thousand Oaks, CA: Corwin, 2018.
Gottschall, Jonathan. *The Storytelling Animal: How Stories Make Us Human.* Boston: Mariner Books, 2013.
Graesser, Arthur C., Murray Singer, and Tom Trabasso. "Constructing Inferences During Narrative Text Comprehension." *Psychological Review* 101, no. 3 (1994): 371–95.
Green, M. C., and T. C. Brock. "In the Mind's Eye. Transportation-Imagery Model of Narrative Persuasion." In *Narrative Impact. Social and Cognitive Foundations,* edited by M. C. Green, J. J. Strange, and T. C. Brock, 315–42. Mahwah, NJ: Erlbaum, 2002.
———. "The Role of Transportation in the Persuasiveness of Public Narratives." *Journal of Personality and Social Psychology* 79, no. 5 (November 2000): 701–21.
Herman, David, James Phelan, Peter J. Rabinowitz, Brian Richardson, and Robyn Warhol. *Narrative Theory: Core Concepts & Critical Debates.* Columbus: The Ohio State University Press, 2012.
Humphries, Debra, and Abigail Davenport. "What Really Matters in College: How Students View and Value Liberal Education: Liberal Education & America's Promise." *Liberal Education* 91, no. 3 (2005): 36–43.
Immordino-Yang, M. H., and A. Damasio. "We Feel, Therefore We Learn: The Relevance of Affective and Social Neuroscience to Education." *Mind, Brain, and Education* 1, no. 1 (2007): 3–10.
Kreuter, Matthew W., Melanie C. Green, Joseph N. Cappella, Michael D. Slater, Meg E. Wise, Doug Storey, Eddie M. Clark, et al. "Narrative Communication in Cancer Prevention and Control: A Framework to Guide Research and Application." *Annals of Behavioral Medicine* 33, no. 3 (September 1, 2007): 221–35.
McKee, Robert. *Story: Style, Structure, Substance, and the Principles of Screenwriting.* New York: Harper Collins, 1997.
McNett, Gabriel. "Using Stories to Facilitate Learning." *College Teaching* 64, no. 4 (2016): 184–93.
Pinker, Steven. *How the Mind Works.* New York: W. W. Norton, 2009.
Sarbin, Theodore R., ed. *Narrative Psychology: The Storied Nature of Human Conduct.* New York: Praeger, 1986.
Schank, Roger C. *Explanation Patterns: Understanding Mechanically and Creatively.* Hillsdale, NJ: L. Erlbaum Associates, 1986.
Slater, M. D. "Entertainment Education and the Persuasive Impact of Narratives." In *Narrative Impact: Social and Cognitive Foundations,* edited by M. C. Green, J. J. Strange, and T. C. Brock, 157–81. Mahwah, NJ: Lawrence Erlbaum Associates, 2002.
Stein, Nancy, Bennett Leventhal, and Tom Trabasso, eds. *Psychological and Biological Approaches to Emotion.* Hilllsdale, NJ: Laurence, Erlbaum Associates, 1990.
Street, Brian V. "What's 'New' in the New Literacy Studies: Current Approaches to Literacy in Theory and Practice." *Current Issues in Comparative Education* 5, no. 2 (1993): 77–91.
Thuna, Mindy, and Joanna Szurmak. "Telling Their Stories: A Study of Librarians' Use of Narrative in Instruction." *Journal of Academic Librarianship* 45, no. 5 (2019): 1–12.
Vossler, Joshua J., and John Watts. "Educational Story as a Tool for Addressing the Framework for Information Literacy for Higher Education." *portal: Libraries and the Academy* 17, no. 3 (July 1, 2017): 529–42.

Chapter 5

Revealing the Means of (Information) Production:

Collaborative Storytelling to Demystify Scholarship

Dunstan McNutt

I was bored. Or, at least, a little burnt out. After teaching mostly introductory composition courses and the like for my first job, my second job at a small liberal arts college opened the opportunities to teach in areas where I had more expertise, namely, in history. But after a few years, I felt like my lesson plans were starting to get recycled and stale. Yes, I incorporated active learning. Yes, I did my best to encourage discussion. But there were only so many ways for me to cover how to find secondary and primary sources in library databases. I needed to do something new, or my boredom was going to be passed along to the faculty with whom I collaborated and, even worse, the students.

73

They were bored. Or at least they expected to be bored. I walked into yet another upper-division history class with a sense of trepidation. Or, to be more honest, dread. Having just arrived in my new position at an institution with a well-established instructional program, I had quickly learned that the history students felt they had learned what they needed to from librarians. Because history classes often have a research component and because the history faculty want to set their students up for success, they often incorporate library instruction into their syllabus. While this is many a humanities librarian's dream—having the opportunity to engage students with in-depth research situated in a particular field of history—students sometimes have difficulty differentiating the content from one class to another. And so, a group of students shuffles in, expecting to be "taught" how to use JSTOR. Again.

Fortunately, a colleague recommended a professional development experience she couldn't say enough positive things about: Dartmouth College Library's Librarians Active Learning Institute. Better yet, they were offering a new track for working with Archives and Special Collections. As I increasingly worked with our own library's A&SC department, this seemed like a perfect opportunity. And it was. I'll never forget gathering around a seminar table with my new colleagues as we each examined an item or two from their special collections, only to have a story unfold as each of us reported back to the larger group. What started as a confusing mess of university records, salacious news stories, and old photos soon became an engrossing narrative about the practice of stealing cadavers for use in the medical school and subsequent policies to show greater respect for bodily donations. This approach to teaching the use of primary sources was anything but boring.

So, imagine the students' surprise when they are broken into groups and, without even being prompted to log in to their computers, are handed a packet of print sources, one per student, along with a handout with questions for source analysis. This particular aspect is nothing new to most of them, and at first they dutifully read their documents (at least most of them do), answer the questions as if a rote exercise, and start to glaze over. But then the mood shifts. They are asked to establish the chronological order of the documents they analyzed and to share their findings in that order. As I scan the room, I see a member of nearly every group light up, shuffling through their document and findings as another student shares their historical anecdote. "But these officials aren't even mentioning the atrocities from my document in 1895! It's like they are looking at the 1918 massacres in a vacuum!"

The activity is meant to make each group a collaborative history lab. Each student is given a piece of a historical puzzle, but they don't have the picture on the box to make sense of their piece until they start hearing from their colleagues. By the end of the fifteen minutes or so, students are (in the best of cases) excitedly creating a timeline and coming up with an interpretation or hypothesis about the evidence in front of them. This is how history is done. This is why their professor wants them to base their arguments on primary sources. This is the hook that (I hope) makes scholarly inquiry and the search for original documents in a myriad of confusing databases and unintuitive interfaces worthwhile.

Full disclosure: some of the students were still bored. But most of them weren't, and I wasn't either.

Storytelling Goal

The general learning outcome I am trying to meet with this teaching method is to provide a demonstration of an authentic information gathering, analysis, and synthesis activity in a limited amount of time. I have found students to have difficulty differentiating between types of sources in our increasingly flattened information landscape, both in how they were originally intended to be used and how they might be used at a later time in the course of scholarly inquiry. This exercise provides a venue in which students are able to work with one another to differentiate between sources, deliberate about how sources might work together, and develop an argument about how they could be interpreted. Viewing this approach through the lens of the ACRL *Framework for Information Literacy for Higher Education*, this activity demonstrates the notion of research as inquiry, giving students practice in synthesizing "ideas gathered from multiple sources."[1] Students are challenged to shift their questions and interpretations in real time as new evidence is brought to light. Although this rarely leaves as much class time for searching for sources, which is often the bread and butter of a library instruction session, I find this gives students a better sense of what kinds of sources they would be searching for, why they would be searching for them, and how they will be used in the proper context. One always has to make choices when prioritizing learning outcomes with time constraints, but the feedback I have received from professors and the level of engagement I see in students has led me to believe this to be a worthwhile trade-off.

Audience

The three contexts in which I have most often used this method are (1) introductory general education courses, wherein we are exploring the information landscape and the varieties of sources students will likely encounter using library resources; (2) introductory history courses, when students are just starting to differentiate between primary and secondary sources and learning other aspects of disciplinary publication practices; and (3) upper-division history courses, where more of an emphasis is being placed on telling a historical narrative and making a primary source-based argument. In each of these cases, I select different sources that are appropriate or related to their coursework and illustrative of the relevant information creation process.

Delivery

Regardless of the audience, my approach to these sessions follows a similar structure: (1) define the learning outcomes; (2) choose a course-appropriate example; (3) choose the relevant sources; and (4) construct a (potential) timeline to illustrate the most important points. What follows are examples of this approach for a variety of audiences. Lesson plan structure, analysis prompts, and sample bibliographies can be found below under "Practical Example."

Introductory General Education Courses

In many introductory general education courses, learning outcomes are tied to students developing a better understanding of the variety of sources they may be encountering for the first time and how those sources are best used in an academic setting. While working at a selective liberal arts college that was experimenting with a summer bridge program for incoming first-year students, I partnered with a faculty member leading a section to provide an introduction to library resources. Though there wasn't a major research paper assigned, students were going to take part in a group debate over the ethics of using cochlear implants in early childhood, and the professor wanted students to seek perspectives beyond their assigned readings. She also wanted students to get a sense of the scope of the library's significant holdings and online resources.

In some situations, choosing the example and the sources are intertwined, as was the case with this session. Using an *Atlantic* article the professor assigned as a starting point, I selected a number of related sources, including newspaper articles from the early development stages of cochlear implants, a congressional hearing on the topic of funding further research, and a more recent article in a philosophy journal exploring ethical dimensions of the issue. Before distributing the sources to groups of four or five, we discussed the BEAM framework for evaluating a source's efficacy, considering how different sources might be better for different research needs (background information, evidence, arguments, or methodologies), and provided a handout with source analysis prompts for students to use with consideration of their individual source.

Prior to the session, I developed the timeline I hoped they would reconstruct and made sure I was ready to fill in gaps where necessary to illustrate the relevant learning outcomes. But first, it was their turn. Students had time on their own with their assigned source, then came together as a small group to share. They put their sources in chronological order, discussed how different sources might be used for a research project, and identified which sources would be most useful for their debate. We then came back together as a whole class and they shared their findings, with different groups focusing on different dimensions of the activity. Some students thought it was interesting to look at the reproductions of historical newspapers, and others were more curious about the differences between scholarly articles and popular sources, such as *The Atlantic*, and how a congressional hearing was a different genre altogether. Regardless, every group was able to put their sources into the correct timeline and articulate how a story develops over time, how technological advances shape ethical conversations, and the legitimate but conflicting perspectives on the issue. Not only were students able to articulate the relative potential utility of different sources and get an introduction to the diversity of the library's collection, but they also appeared to have a good time while they were learning. It was my hope that having a low-stakes, engaging activity would reduce any anxiety incoming students might feel toward a potentially overwhelming library, depending on prior experiences in libraries.[2]

In other introductory courses, faculty might want students to gain an understanding of a particular form of academic writing so they are able to better develop their own approach to writing for a scholarly audience. In one such course, I collaborated with a First-Year Seminar professor to develop a session on the way literary criticism is written and how scholars engage with fiction as primary sources to construct their own arguments. To use the language of the *Framework*, scholarship can be viewed as a conversation, but this threshold concept is difficult for students to grasp and can be challenging to illustrate in an obvious way.[3]

With these learning outcomes in mind, and being mindful that the course was drawing heavily from Russian literature, I chose my example and sources:

- excerpts from Dostoevsky's *The Brothers Karamazov*;
- excerpts from David Foster Wallace's *Infinite Jest*;
- an essay written by Wallace about Dostoevsky;
- a work of criticism connecting the influence of Shakespeare's *Hamlet* to *Infinite Jest*; and
- a work of criticism arguing *Hamlet* was less important to Wallace than *The Brothers Karamazov*.

It should be noted that David Foster Wallace was an alum of this institution, and there was a great deal of reverence and pride in this fact among the student body (more on this below under "Cultural Considerations").

My timeline was thus constructed to provide an overview of the relevant publication dates and the ways in which evidence accumulated such that scholars could incorporate them into their own writing. The above examples illustrated how an author might frame their disagreement with a scholar that came before them and provide the evidence both were drawing from so students could weigh in on the relative merits of the different interpretations.

This exercise led to a lively discussion of the way the scholars used their evidence and the practical stylistic choices they made in framing their arguments. This model would work for any discipline that has discreet practices around how researchers write with sources, whether they be primary or secondary. In my experience, it is rarely difficult to find examples of scholars disagreeing with one another over the same source material, as was the case with the above selections.

Introductory History Courses

When collaborating with departmental faculty, I try to zoom out on the larger curriculum of the major and scaffold my learning outcomes accordingly. At my current institution, I am fortunate to have an introductory history class that all majors are required to take before proceeding to upper-division courses. I have attempted to standardize the structure of this class, so all students in upper-division courses have a foundation of the ways in which historians use primary sources and produce scholarship. From the original sources upon which histories are written to the interpretations of those sources in secondary sources to the reception of that scholarship in book reviews and historiographies, students must grapple with analyzing these sources to better understand the original context in which they were produced. Further, they must understand how they might use these different sources in the context of writing history: when to read a source as evidence, when to read a source for the arguments, and how to strategically use scholarly conventions to find other sources and evaluate them.

An example that has worked particularly well this year, on the one-hundredth anniversary of women's suffrage being achieved in the United States, spans two class periods: one in a traditional library classroom, and one in UTC's Special Collections. The first session is intended to demonstrate the arc of historical research: students are introduced to both primary and secondary sources, popular and scholarly sources, and a book review. For primary sources, students are given a political ad opposing women's suffrage and a newspaper editorial in *The Tennessean* supporting women's right to vote. Another student reads a brief article for a popular audience on Tennessee's role in passing the Nineteenth Amendment, including an illustration of the political ad analyzed by their classmate. A scholarly article delves into the alliance between suffragists and African American women in Nashville, and a book review puts two edited volumes on women's suffrage in conversation with one another and contextualizes them in the larger historiography.

These examples are meant to show students new to the academic study of history the range of sources they should encounter in their research: different types of primary sources with different perspectives and rhetorical strategies, different types of secondary sources with different audiences and purposes in mind, and some of the elements of scholarship that might seem obvious to a practitioner that has likely never been encountered by a novice. Not only are students able to tell a story about how the different sources likely came to exist and work in relationship with one another, they are also able to discuss strategies for finding these kinds of sources and how they might be springboards to other useful materials on the same topic. Further, it sets them up for a day in Special Collections where they can focus solely on primary sources held by the institution and try their own hands at developing a historical narrative.

In collaboration with Carolyn Runyon, director of Special Collections at UTC Library, part two of this class sequence uses materials from the University Archives, such as the student newspaper, *UTC Echo*, the Chattanooga History Collections[4] (a partnership with Chattanooga Public Library housed at UTC), and the Marilyn Lloyd Papers,[5] a collection of materials from the first congresswoman from Tennessee. The materials range from 1908 to 1993 and are meant to illustrate the complicated gender dynamics of political participation in the twentieth-century United States and in Tennessee specifically. While students encounter evidence of women's active participation in politics, both in gaining the right to vote and achieving political representation in Congress, they are also challenged to consider how men have taken credit for these achievements, and how women have pragmatically navigated political realities. This is admittedly a difficult task for students who are not only encountering archival materials for the first time but also developing historical arguments from primary evidence without a great deal of practice. We have found students are able to get a foothold in the process, which helps facilitate a productive and engaging discussion to meet the learning objectives. We close by tying the two classes together and talk about how the sources they encounter in Special Collections are the kinds of sources scholars used to write the secondary sources they looked at the previous week in the library classroom.

Upper-division History Courses

By the time students get to upper-division history courses, their professors have an expectation that they will be relying heavily on primary sources to develop an original historical argument. And yet, in my discussion with faculty and students alike, it is rarely obvious where students would have learned to develop that rather sophisticated skill. It is one thing for a professor or librarian to point a student toward an archival collection or digital surrogate, but it is difficult for students to see how what they are doing for a research assignment is comparable to what the scholars they have been reading are doing in their articles and books. There is a tacit understanding that the books and articles they are reading are telling them what happened in the past, but it is less clear that scholars are making decisions about what documents they use to construct a narrative and that they apply an interpretive lens to those documents in developing their own arguments.

For upper-division classes, my learning outcomes are tied to this practice of synthesizing information and developing historical arguments. Illustrating this disciplinary practice in a classroom setting makes the process more concrete and manageable. Having read and analyzed sources on their own, pieced together a timeline with their colleagues based on their findings, and then developed a hypothesis about how the sources work together, they feel better prepared to do this work on their own as they dig into a topic of their choosing. Furthermore, the librarian and disciplinary faculty can demonstrate how the sources that were chosen were not the only sources available, what the sources looked like in their original organization or context, and how decisions were made to nudge students toward a potential narrative and interpretation.

In a recent iteration of a capstone history course, wherein students are required to write a fifteen- to twenty-page paper drawing heavily from primary sources, the disciplinary faculty decided to confine students to topics on the diplomatic history of the Middle East discussed in the State Department's *Foreign Relations of the United States*, made available through the

University of Wisconsin's Digital Collections.[6] This was the first encounter most students had with this extensive collection of primary sources, so we planned a series of library instruction sessions designed to familiarize them with the types of sources they would encounter over the course of their research: the first focused on developing historical arguments from primary sources and identifying problematic aspects of available source material, the second provided students an opportunity to explore the digital collections, and a final session covered searching for and accessing secondary sources.

Given the emphasis of the course, my choice of examples and sources was much more manageable than some other open-ended research methods courses. I selected sources that told a story about the Armenian genocide and highlighted the ways in which *FRUS* provides a US-centered perspective on foreign policy, even if it includes the voices of other diplomats. Starting with documents from the 1895 riots and subsequent massacre of Armenians, each group then traced accounts of the 1918 genocide, Washington's initial support for an Armenian state, and subsequent inaction following the Paris Peace Conference. Students were supplied with a primary source analysis handout and a cheat sheet for accessing, searching, and citing *FRUS*. Each group did an excellent job developing a thesis interpreting the available evidence, and these documents provided a solid foundation for a discussion on the editorial process involved in the State Department's publications as well as my own decision-making process in selecting the documents used in the exercise. Subsequent correspondence with my faculty collaborator indicated that the final papers demonstrated the students' ability to bring primary source evidence to bear on their research questions. This felt like a vindication, as the higher-order thinking involved in using information found in research had often been underemphasized in service to the more mechanical aspects of searching for information, even though the former was a higher priority to faculty and a bigger challenge to students.

Theory

Early in my career, Chip and Dan Heath's *Made to Stick* provided inspiration as I developed my approach to teaching. One of the chapters I found most compelling, however, was the one I had the most difficulty applying in the classroom. Chapter 6, Stories, discusses how to use stories as simulation (telling people how to act) and as inspiration (giving people energy to act).[7] This is part of why the experience at Dartmouth was such a revelation. As the previous examples have hopefully shown, this model of collaboratively creating stories of scholarship helps students know how to do research—and energizes them to do so. It thus relates to two theoretical underpinnings: the role storytelling plays in memory and retention, illustrating a constructivist approach to learning, and the way expectation and surprise can add an emotional component to the learning experience, improving engagement.

A recent review of the literature on the benefits of using stories and storytelling in teaching echoes the recommendations of *Made to Stick*: teaching with stories provides a structure for remembering course material, helps create interest, shares information in a recognizable form, and connects teachers with their students.[8] The approach I have discussed thus far connects more to the first two aspects.[9] Having a better understanding of how teaching with stories improves both retention and engagement might help structure the learning experience.

Constructivism as an educational theory has informed many teaching librarians' approaches to information literacy instruction, and the idea that learners rely on past experience in order to assimilate new knowledge fits nicely with the model of teaching that has been discussed. Summarizing the research on the connection between narrative and memory, Schank and Berman describe learning as being constituted by "the modification of our memory structures, our mental representations."[10] This modification is made possible by the stories we tell:

> Each time we tell the story, that telling becomes our most recent memory of the event. The more times we tell it a particular way the more it becomes our memory of the event…. In other words, our story formation becomes our memory formation as well. We remember stories by telling them, and when we tell stories, we shape what we remember.[11]

This is often seen as a nefarious aspect of storytelling, that our memories are not to be trusted because they are not necessarily representative of what *actually* happened, but rather, the story *we tell* about what happened. The upshot of this, however, in the context of teaching, is that motivating students to become active participants in the storytelling process improves the chances of retention. When structured thoughtfully, with the intended outcomes in mind and the right examples chosen, students are given an opportunity to internalize the structure of scholarly discourse through a shared experience with fellow learners.

Not only does storytelling help with the retention of content, but it can also be motivating. In a quote that so accurately describes my experience at Dartmouth and the response I have seen from students in the classroom, Green describes our connection to storytelling: "Students are awake, following along, wanting to find out what happens next and how the story ends."[12] This feels especially true when you have one piece of the puzzle and you are waiting to hear what the other people in your group have or when something someone else shares connects to the clues you have at your disposal. The jigsaw structure of lesson plans described above provides an opportunity to create what the Heaths refer to as a "gap in knowledge" or a stimulus for curiosity.[13] When you have a piece of information out of context, you are naturally inclined to fit it into a larger story, to make meaning out of it. Indeed, "in the teaching context, a storyteller can present material as a mystery, and students will be naturally inclined to 'figure out' the story, thus engaging in the process of sensemaking."[14] Curiosity is a difficult emotion to artificially inspire, but I have found even a semi-engaged class to be receptive to this prompting in the variety of contexts described above.

Cultural Considerations

I take the cultural considerations of this approach to teaching to be twofold: enculturating students into a disciplinary mindset with which they may not be familiar and attempting to provide culturally relevant (and sensitive) content in the examples we choose as educators. In terms of the former, I try to be transparent with students about the fact that scholarly conventions are somewhat arbitrary but important to consider when wanting one's work to be taken seriously. While in an ideal world I would hope that students would be prepared to challenge such conventions with a critical mindset, I also recognize that there are benefits to aligning one's writing with the expectations of the reader. It is my hope that this approach to teaching is capable of making both motivations clear.

As for the opportunity of providing culturally relevant and sensitive content in the class setting, I have cause to reflect on this due to my own failures. Two examples come to mind: using David Foster Wallace as an example in an introductory college course and using a peer-reviewed article that promotes the use of cochlear implants in the context of the other sources under consideration. As for the first, if I were to do this class session over again, I would not use the David Foster Wallace example. For one thing, I could have taken this opportunity to draw attention to scholarship focusing on literary figures outside of a predominantly white, male canon. More importantly, I originally taught this class when I was unaware of the controversy surrounding Wallace's abusive treatment of Mary Karr.[15] In increasingly diverse classrooms, we should take advantage of the opportunities to include traditionally marginalized literary voices and how they are discussed in scholarship.[16] I would also not want to use this example without discussing the problematic aspects of Wallace's biography, which would be outside the scope of the learning objectives agreed upon with the faculty partner for this class.

When selecting sources for lesson plans such as those discussed thus far, one must be mindful of how they work together, and what perspectives might be privileged. Reflecting on the introductory college course that discussed the ethics of cochlear implants, I realized that the only scholarly, peer-reviewed source I chose was arguing for the use of cochlear implants against the position predominant in the Deaf community. Although this did not come up in discussion, in retrospect, I recognize that students could take this perspective to be more authoritative, as it is coming from a scholarly rather than popular source. In recent years, I have found students to be increasingly skeptical of traditional journalistic outlets, and I make more of an effort to consider the potential weight students might give scholarly sources.

Practical Example
Lesson Plan

The following is a guide for creating an activity relevant to your teaching context, along with prompts you might have students use to interrogate their sources and construct their timelines in groups. You will also find sample bibliographies of sources used in the above examples.

1. Define your desired learning outcome. Your sources should not only tell a story but also illustrate the relevant information literacy concept or disciplinary convention that will help students in their own research. *What does the information landscape look like in a given field? What are the patterns of scholarly conversations you want students to understand? What are the types of sources with which you want students to be familiar?*

2. Choose an example. Identify a topic relevant to the course material that would make for a good story. *Is there an assigned reading from a class syllabus that you could deconstruct with sources? Is there a rich disciplinary narrative with which you're already familiar? Are there library resources or online collections you want to highlight in your instruction?*

3. Choose your sources. Identify a variety of sources (4–6) that represent different genres or conventions within the chosen discipline. *Are there particular sources that students should be incorporating into their own research? Can you find sources that are explicitly referenced in your other examples?*

4. Construct your timeline. When students report their findings, you will want to have an ideal timeline prepared so you can fill any relevant gaps. Be prepared for students to highlight details or takeaways you didn't anticipate, as this will often lead to more engaging discussions. *What key concepts or formats are represented by individual sources? How does the story unfold over time? What are important thematic elements or disciplinary conventions illustrated by the sources taken together?*

Sample Source Analysis Prompts for Handouts/Slides

Date of production and/or publication

Author, creator, and/or publisher

Intended audience: *Who do you think was meant to read this source originally?*

Type of source/nature of publication: *Is this a primary or secondary source? What kind of source is it? Don't worry if you aren't sure, or if you aren't familiar with this type of publication, just make an educated guess based on available clues.*

Evidence or information to be drawn from this source: *How would you describe this source to someone who has not read it? What are important themes or arguments?*

Question formulation: *What questions does your source raise? What might help you better contextualize this source?*

Sample Bibliographies

Context: Introductory courses to demonstrate information landscape
Topic: Ethics of cochlear implants in early childhood

Dolnick, Edward. "Deafness as Culture." *The Atlantic* 272, no. 3 (September 1993): 37–53.

Freese, Arthur S. "An Implant Pierces Walls of Deafness." *Boston Globe* (June 10, 1979).

Levy, Neil. "Reconsidering Cochlear Implants: The Lessons of Martha's Vineyard." *Bioethics* 16, no. 2 (April 2002): 134–53.

Schmeck, Jr., Harold M. "Implant Brings Sound to Deaf and Spurs Debate Over Its Use." *New York Times* (March 27, 1984).

U.S. Congress. Joint Economic Committee. *Biotechnology Summit: Putting a Human Face on Biotechnology*, 106th Cong. September 29, 1999.

Context: First-year seminar looking at literary criticism
Topic: Dostoevsky's influence on David Foster Wallace's *Infinite Jest*

Boswell, Marshall. *Understanding David Foster Wallace*. Columbia, SC: University of South Carolina Press, 2009, 165–68.

Dostoyevsky, Fyodor. *The Brothers Karamazov*. Translated by Constance Garnett. New York: Random House, 1933, 287–88, 300–02.

Jacobs, Timothy. "The Brothers Incandenza: Translating Ideology in Fyodor Dostoevsky's *The Brothers Karamazov* and David Foster Wallace's *Infinite Jest*." *Texas Studies in Literature and Language; Austin* 49, no. 3 (Fall 2007): 265–92.

Wallace, David Foster. "Feodor's Guide." *The Village Voice*. April 9, 1996: 15–16.

———. *Infinite Jest*. Boston: Little, Brown and Company, 1996, 39–42.

Context: Introductory history courses, part 1: demonstrate information landscape; part 2: demonstrate archival collections
Topic: Women's suffrage

PART 1

Goodstein, Anita. "A Rare Alliance: African American and White Women in the Tennessee Elections of 1919 and 1920." *The Journal of Southern History* 64, no. 2 (1998): 219–46.

Nashville Tennessean. "Committee Reports Suffrage Favorably: Recommends Ratification Resolution Be Adopted by Members of Lower House." August 17, 1920.

Newman, Judith. "Mother Knew Best." *American History* 45, no. 4 (2010): 34–35.

Southern Women's League for the Rejection of the Susan B. Anthony Amendment. "America When Feminized." Broadside, 1920. Josephine A. Pearson Papers, 1860–1943. Tennessee State Library and Archives. https://teva.contentdm.oclc.org/digital/collection/p15138coll27/id/6.

Wolfe, Margaret Ripley. "Review of *Votes for Women! The Woman Suffrage Movement in Tennessee, the South, and the Nation; One Woman, One Vote: Rediscovering the Woman Suffrage Movement*." *The Journal of American History* 83, no. 3 (1996): 1032–33.

PART 2

University of Tennessee. All sources. Chattanooga, Special Collections:
Business Woman's Suffrage Club of Chattanooga. Annual Suffrage Demonstration program. May 2, 1916. CHC-2003-011-005. Box: CHC D156.
Fisher, Anna A. "The Proof of the Pudding." *University Echo*, vol. 10, no. 2. (November 5, 1915): 3–4. LH1 .C75.
I'm Proud of Marilyn. Bumper sticker, circa 1975–1995. Box: MS-025 199.
"Joint Debate." *University Echo*, vol. 3, no. 4 (December 1, 1908): 16. LH1 .C75.
Lloyd, Marilyn. National Association of Bank Women. Speech, April 16, 1990. Box: MS-025 126.
Marilyn Lloyd is My Congresswoman. Bumper sticker, circa 1975–1995. Box: MS-025 199.
McMinn County Chapter of the East Tennessee Historical Society meeting announcement. January 3, 1965. CHC-2004-018-568-a. Box: CHC H007.
Mrs. Mort Lloyd. Button, circa 1975–1995. Box: MS-025 199.
Sandra S. Perkinson correspondence with Marilyn Lloyd. October 7, 1993. Box: MS-025 199.
Tennessee Equal Suffrage Association. Photograph, circa 1912. CHC-1990-048-001. Box: CHC PF008.

Context: Upper-division history class demonstrating the use of primary sources
Topic: Armenian genocide
"Instructions for Commissioners from the Peace Conference, March 25, 1919." In *Papers Relating to the Foreign Relations of the United States, The Paris Peace Conference, 1919*, 12: 745–47. Washington: Government Printing Office, 1919.
Lansing. "The Secretary of State to the Ambassador of Great Britain (Davis), Washington, August 26, 1919." In *Papers Relating to the Foreign Relations of the United States, 1919*, 2: 836–37. Washington: Government Printing Office, 1919.
Nubar, Boghos. "The President of the Armenian National Delegation (Nubar) to President Wilson." In *Papers Relating to the Foreign*

Relations of the United States, 1918. Supplement I, The World War, 1: 886–87. Washington: Government Printing Office, 1918.

Phillips. "The Acting Secretary of State to the Commission to Negotiate Peace, Washington, June 28, 1919." In *Papers Relating to the Foreign Relations of the United States, 1919*, 2: 824. Washington: Government Printing Office, 1919.

Polk. "The Acting Secretary of State to the Ambassador in France (Wallace), Washington, January 24, 1920." In *Papers Relating to the Foreign Relations of the United States, 1920*, 3: 775–76. Washington: Government Printing Office, 1920.

———. "The Acting Secretary of State to the Ambassador in France (Wallace), Washington, January 27, 1920." In *Papers Relating to the Foreign Relations of the United States, 1920*, 3: 776–77. Washington: Government Printing Office, 1920.

Terrell, A. W. "Legation of the United States, Constantinople, October 3, 1895." In *Foreign Relations of the United States, 1895*, 2: 1318–19. Washington: Government Printing Office, 1895.

"The Ambassador in Turkey (Morgenthau) to the Secretary of State, Constantinople, July 10, 1915." In *Papers Relating to the Foreign Relations of the United States, 1915. Supplement, The World War*, 982–84. Washington: Government Printing Office, 1915.

Context: Upper-division history course to demonstrate scholarship as a conversation

Topic: U.S. involvement in 1953 coup in Iran

Byrne, Malcolm, ed. "Iran 1953: State Department Finally Releases Updated Official History of Mosaddeq Coup." National Security Archive, June 15, 2017. https://nsarchive.gwu.edu/briefing-book/iran/2017-06-15/iran-1953-state-department-finally-releases-updated-official-history.

Doty, Robert C. "New Regime in Iran Opens War on Reds; Prince Is Arrested." *New York Times* (August 25, 1953).

Gasiorowski, Mark J. "The 1953 Coup D'etat in Iran." *International Journal of Middle East Studies* 19, no. 3 (1987): 261–86.

Raether, Carl N., and Charles S. Sampson, eds. "Statement of Policy Proposed by the National Security Council: November 1952." In

Foreign Relations of the United States, 1952–1954, Iran, 1951–1954, X:529–34. Washington: Government Printing Office, 1989. https://history.state.gov/historicaldocuments/frus1952-54v10/d240.

Razi, G. Hossein. Review of *Mohammad Mosaddeq and the 1953 Coup in Iran*, by Mark J. Gasiorowski and Malcolm Byrne. *International Journal of Middle East Studies* 41, no. 1 (2009): 176–78.

Endnotes

1. *Framework for Information Literacy for Higher Education*, Association of College and Research Libraries (ACRL), 2015, http://www.ala.org/acrl/standards/ilframework.
2. The final section of the chapter, "Lesson plans and bibliographies" includes citations for this and subsequent examples.
3. *Framework*, Association of College and Research Libraries.
4. "Chattanooga History Collections Online," University of Tennessee Chattanooga and Chattanooga Public Library, n.d., Chattanooga History Collections Online, https://www.utc.edu/library/special-collections/collections/chattanooga-history-collections.php.
5. "Marilyn Lloyd Papers," University of Tennessee, Chattanooga, n.d., MS-025, UTC Library Special Collections, https://findingaids.library.utc.edu/repositories/2/resources/105.
6. "Foreign Relations of the United States," University of Wisconsin-Madison Libraries, University of Wisconsin Digital Collections, n.d., http://digital.library.wisc.edu/1711.dl/FRUS.
7. Chip Heath, *Made to Stick: Why Some Ideas Survive and Others Die*, 1st ed. (New York: Random House, 2007), 204–37.
8. R. Eric Landrum, Karen Brakke, and Maureen A. McCarthy, "The Pedagogical Power of Storytelling," *Scholarship of Teaching and Learning in Psychology [Advance Online Publication]* 5, no. 3 (September 2019): 2, http://dx.doi.org.proxy.lib.utc.edu/10.1037/stl0000152.
9. Though perhaps out of the scope of this chapter, this practice also has a connection to the last aspect: teaching librarians develop better empathy for students embarking on a research project after having gone through the experience of gathering course-relevant materials using the platforms on which students will have to rely.
10. Roger C. Schank and Tamara R. Berman, "The Pervasive Role of Stories in Knowledge and Action," in *Narrative Impact: Social and Cognitive Foundations*, ed. Melanie C. Green, Jeffrey J. Strange, and Timothy C. Brock (New York: Psychology Press, 2013), 302.
11. Schank and Berman, "The Pervasive Role of Stories," 290.
12. Melanie C. Green, "Storytelling in Teaching," *APS Observer* (blog), April 2004, https://www.psychologicalscience.org/observer/storytelling-in-teaching.
13. Heath, *Made to Stick*, 84–85.
14. Landrum, Brakke, and McCarthy, "The Pedagogical Power of Storytelling," 3.
15. Megan Garber, "David Foster Wallace and the Dangerous Romance of Male Genius," *The Atlantic*, May 9, 2018, https://www.theatlantic.com/entertainment/archive/2018/05/the-world-still-spins-around-male-genius/559925/.

16. To this point, I am indebted to a thoughtful commenter in an evaluation of my LOEX presentation that used this example.

Bibliography

Association of College and Research Libraries. *Framework for Information Literacy for Higher Education."* Association of College & Research Libraries (ACRL), 2015. http://www.ala.org/acrl/standards/ilframework.

Garber, Megan. "David Foster Wallace and the Dangerous Romance of Male Genius." *The Atlantic* (May 9, 2018). https://www.theatlantic.com/entertainment/archive/2018/05/the-world-still-spins-around-male-genius/559925/.

Green, Melanie C. "Storytelling in Teaching." *APS Observer* (blog), April 2004. https://www.psychologicalscience.org/observer/storytelling-in-teaching.

Heath, Chip. *Made to Stick: Why Some Ideas Survive and Others Die.* 1st ed. New York: Random House, 2007.

Landrum, R. Eric, Karen Brakke, and Maureen A. McCarthy. "The Pedagogical Power of Storytelling." *Scholarship of Teaching and Learning in Psychology [Advance Online Publication]* 5, no. 3 (September 2019): 1–7. http://dx.doi.org.proxy.lib.utc.edu/10.1037/stl0000152.

Schank, Roger C., and Tamara R. Berman. "The Pervasive Role of Stories in Knowledge and Action." In *Narrative Impact: Social and Cognitive Foundations*, edited by Melanie C. Green, Jeffrey J. Strange, and Timothy C. Brock, 287–313. New York: Psychology Press, 2013.

University of Tennessee, Chattanooga. "Marilyn Lloyd Papers," n.d. MS-025. UTC Library Special Collections. https://findingaids.library.utc.edu/repositories/2/resources/105.

University of Tennessee, Chattanooga, and Chattanooga Public Library. "Chattanooga History Collections Online," n.d. Chattanooga History Collections Online.

University of Wisconsin-Madison Libraries. "Foreign Relations of the United States." University of Wisconsin Digital Collections, n.d. http://digital.library.wisc.edu/1711.dl/FRUS.

Chapter 6

The Depository Is Large. It Contains Multitudes

L. E. Eames

A fresh-faced, first-year MLIS student sits down at his office desk at his student library job and cracks open a hard-cover, linen-bound journal. It is… February? January? Hard to say. It's been raining since daylight time ended. And to be fair, you can't see the sky from the office that once belonged to some other unit but has slowly but surely been ceded to the graduate student employees to no real complaints from anyone. The young grad student picks up a blue pen and begins a list in his journal:

> US LGBTQ History
> - Military Service: DADT, Trans Service Ban
> - Blood bans (AIDS in gov docs)
> - Bathroom Bills
> - Lavender Scare
> - Marriage/Civil Rights (via SCOTUS?)
>   ** UN Intersex Stats Doc

In the background, a kettle dings to indicate that water has boiled. The other gov pubs grad student employee enters, a fresh cup of tea in her hand. Looking up at his colleague, he leans back in his chair and looks over his shoulder. "Hey there, friend...."

"What's up?" she says, placing the cup of tea on her desk and tossing her planner beside it.

"Can I talk through a thing?" he asks.

"Sure."

"Ok. So. I'm reworking the Gays in the Military Guide, and—."

"Oh good."

"Yeah, like, right. There are other stories we could be telling on that page... there's more than just the military. But—."

"YES."

"But let's say I put together this 'Queer Americans' identity oriented LibGuide ...something-something. Which is what I want because if the Gays in the Military guide is so popular, there's clearly an audience. And we have the Native Americans page on the Sources by Subject page, right? So, shouldn't we have broader representation there? Do one, do 'em all, you know? Or, well not all—. All is probably impossible. But at least do more."

She sips her tea. "That sounds great."

"Except how much do you do? And what are the divisions?"

"And how do you keep it current?"

"Oof, yeah, how do you keep it current? ...Although maybe if the focus is 'stories' that frames the guide away from the current events."

She squints a little. "How do you mean?"

"I mean... ok, how about blood donation? If we're just thinking about the LGBTQ+ guide for now, how would you frame the gay blood ban? Because that's a great opportunity to talk about US *and* international docs and is a thing that could change in the future. Well, *should* change in the future. Anyway, if you frame it around the story of how we got here, then it's more ok if it gets out of date. Because the focus is on why it was done, not the current state of affairs, it needs less immediate updating if things change."

"Mmmmmk, but then how do you divide it?"

"Right. Yes. Telling every story about everyone in American history is a catchy concept, but that's not, like, actually possible in a LibGuide."

"Weren't we talking about person spotlights for the different heritage months recently?" she asks.

"Ah, yeah, we were, weren't we? Heritage Months could be a good scaffold."

"That would be thematically relevant. Heritage Months are nationally recognized."

"Yes! OK. Yes!" He spins his chair and starts scribbling in the journal again.

"Don't—. You gotta put some scope on this," she comments.

He runs his hand through his hair, breaking off the furious scribbling for a moment. "Oh yeah, no, for sure. But I gotta brainstorm first. I can cut it back later…."

Storytelling Goal

To create a portal centered on reflecting the diverse University of Washington (UW) community in their depository collection and to highlight the variety of ways to research with government documents.

Audience

UW affiliates and Seattle community members looking for starting points for their research with government documents. In particular, these guides are geared toward US Federal documents research. Our unit serves primarily the campus community of students, faculty, and staff, but we also work with area middle and high school students for history day and have a handful of regular public patrons who use our collection. I discuss scope in more depth under "Theory" below, but the main audience is users looking to *start* their research.

Delivery

The Who We Are: Diversity in Government Documents guides are included in the larger Government Sources by Subject LibGuide. The guide is divided into seven tabs: African Americans, Asian Americans and Pacific Islanders, Jewish Americans, Latinx Americans, LGBTQ+ Americans, Muslim Americans, and Women.[1] Each tab includes some basic reference sources, recommended databases for further research, data sources, links to relevant oral history projects, and links to any advocacy groups that seek to represent the needs of the group represented in a given tab. The bulk of the pages are what I called "spotlighted stories." These form the scaffolding of the project.

Even after setting the scope of the guides around the seven identity groups I chose, I had to limit the content of the pages to make the project manageable. By defining my audience as people generally looking for a direction within gov docs, either because they had a passing curiosity or because they were starting a project, I was able to rein in the number of resources I included in each spotlight. I didn't have to include everything, just enough to get someone going. This choice also opened the opportunity to include some non-governmental literature as well as a handful of brief introductory paragraphs that I wrote myself. I used these to fill in the gaps in the government documents. For example, in the spotlight on the US-Mexico border, I included a collection of letters from the Mexican-American War and an episode of *99% Invisible* alongside the Treaty of Guadalupe Hidalgo, a National Parks Service pamphlet on the Chamizal National Memorial, and the Secure Fence Act of 2006. These non-governmental resources serve both to highlight what the government documents didn't cover as well as to provide further research pathways.[2]

Theory

My guiding structural principles in putting together these guides were "timeless currency" and "starting points only." I wanted to ensure that the guide didn't need constant updating. Where possible, I linked to resources that would be updated by other people. This was especially useful in the Representation Spotlights, where I could link to sites such as the Congressional Black and Asian Pacific American Caucuses. This also led to a more historical stance than I had originally planned on taking. It's hard to say what current documents will be considered important, in retrospect, but I tried to choose items from the present day that felt emblematic of policy, with the idea that hopefully they wouldn't have to be replaced as stories evolve. In other cases, I deferred to more historical documents only. On the Reproductive Rights spotlight on the Women page, I used a judicial lens, which allowed me to show how the issue evolved through the lens of government literature but also meant that the spotlight would not require updating in the same way that pointing to legislation would. After all, more cases may be argued in the future, but the texts of *Griswold v. Connecticut*, *Roe v. Wade*, or *Planned Parenthood v. Casey* themselves will remain the same.[3] I also point to resources like Wikipedia that track policy change by country or by state—for instance, "Abortion by Country" and "List of Countries with their stand on MSM [men who have sex with men] blood donors"—to show how these issues continue to develop, with the caveat that users should double-check those lists with their own research.

Cultural Considerations

The source material in this project—government documents—frequently do not reflect a positive, inclusive history for people of minoritized identities. I felt it was critical to present the history of events like the annexation of The Philippines, the US/Mexico border, or blood donation bans in a way that honestly presented the primary sources but which was also respectful to affected communities. I chose the key images for each tab with these principles of respect and honesty in mind. I wanted to select an image that related to one of the stories told on the page and which was in some way celebratory or active. I wanted to avoid overly historicizing these identities. For example, for the LGBTQ+ Americans page, I chose Stonewall at Pride the year it was declared a National Monument.[4] For the Muslim Americans page, I chose an image of the oldest, continuously operating mosque in America from the National Register of Historic Places.

Chapter 6
Practical Examples

Figure 6.1
The home page of the guides.

The Border

Even though the US has a land border with Mexico and with Canada, when we say "The Border" we rarely mean the northern one. Here are a few resources to dip your toes in to understand this immensely complicated issue.

The Borderlands by Andrew G. Wood (Editor) 🛈
Call Number: eBook
ISBN: 9780313339967
Publication Date: 2008

Echoes of the Mexican-American War by Jesus Velasco Marques (Editor); Krystyna Libura (Editor); Luis Gerardo Morales Moreno (Editor); Mark Fried (Translator) 🛈
Call Number: E404 .M83 2004
ISBN: 9780888995827
Publication Date: 2005

Chronicles of the gringos: the U.S. Army in the Mexican War, 1846-1848; accounts of eyewitnesses & combatants. by George Winston Smith Charles B. (Charles Burnet) Judah, 1902-1975.
Call Number: E411 .S6
Publication Date: 1986

The early sentiment for the annexation of California : an account of the growth of American interest in California, 1835-1846. by Robert Glass Cleland, 1885-1957
Call Number: F864 .C63 1915

Annexation of Texas ; opinions of Messrs. Clay, Polk, Benton & Van Buren, on the immediate annexation of Texas.
Publication Date: 1844

Treaty of Guadalupe Hidalgo
Publication Date: 1848

- **99% Invisible - The Border Wall**
  In part 1 of the show, the folks over at The Radio Diaries tell two stories from the Chamizal Dispute. In Part 2, Avery Trufelman examines some of the prototypes for Trump's Wall.

Statecraft, Domestic Politics and Foreign Policy Making by Alan C. Lamborn; Stephen P. Mumme
Call Number: F786 .L28 1988
ISBN: 9780813372914
Publication Date: 1988-05-08

Figure 6.2
The Border. This is an example of a spotlighted story including government info but also other sources where they add richness to the content.

> **Reproductive Rights**
>
> The ability, or lack thereof, to access the full range of choice about family planning options doesn't just affect cisgender women, but it does usually get grouped under "women's issues." It's important to remember that not every person with a uterus is a woman, despite the cisnormative language prevalent in these discussions.
>
> - **Historical & Multicultural Encyclopedia of Female Reproductive Rights In the United States**
>
> Access to Contraception
>
> - **Comstock Laws**
>   Wikipedia provides an excellent aggregation of different Comstock Laws. Comstock Laws were a series of state and federal laws passed under the Grant Administration inspired by the lobbying efforts of Anthony Comstock. The act criminalized the use of the Postal Service for the purpose of sending obscenity, contraceptives, abortifacients, sex toys, personal letters with any sexual content or information, or any information regarding the aforementioned.
> - **The Margaret Sanger Papers Project**
> - Microform: The Margaret Sanger Papers
>   For the Smith College Archival collection see **Microfilm A9492**. For Additional Papers, see **Microfilm A9572** in the Suzzallo Microfilm Collection.
> - **Griswold v. Connecticut (1965)**
>   C. Lee Buxton (a gynecologist) and Estelle Griswold (head of Connecticut Planned Parenthood) were prosecuted under Connecticut's 1879 Comstock Law for opening a Planned Parenthood in New Haven. The Law banned the use of any drug, device, or instrument for contraception. The challenge was based on the **fourteenth amendment**, while the victory centered more on Justice Douglas' interpretation of a right to privacy in the "penumbras" of the **first** and **fifth** amendments.
> - **Eisenstadt v. Baird (1972)**
>   Based on Griswold and the Equal Protection Clause of the fourteenth amendment, this case decided in favor of unmarried people having the same access to contraception as married people.
>
> Access to Abortion
>
> In the United States, the access to abortion procedures is currently protected by the Supreme Court's decision in Roe v. Wade.
>
> - **Roe v. Wade (1971)**
>   Roe wanted to terminate her pregnancy by abortion, which was prohibited by Texas law except in situations to save the life of the pregnant person. The court held 7-2 that the right to an abortion fell within the right to privacy (recognized in Griswold) protected by the fourteenth amendment and that this right gave the pregnant person total autonomy in the first trimester and defined levels of interest and intervention for the second and third trimesters.

Figure 6.3

By focusing on the court cases that shaped the fight for reproductive rights, the guide remains relevant without needing constant updating.

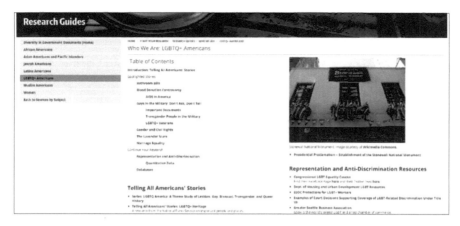

Figure 6.4
This shows both how the table of contents is formatted and the kind of image I chose for each page.

Endnotes

1. L. E. Eames, "Library Guides: Who We Are: Diversity in Government Documents: Home," University Libraries, University of Washington, February 8, 2018, https://guides.lib.uw.edu/research/whoweare/home.
2. L. E. Eames, "Library Guides: Who We Are: Latinx Americans," University Libraries, University of Washington, February 8, 2018, https://guides.lib.uw.edu/research/whoweare/LatinxAmericans.
3. L. E. Eames, "Library Guides: Who We Are: Women," University Libraries, University of Washington, February 8, 2018, https://guides.lib.uw.edu/research/whoweare/WomenInAmerica.
4. L. E. Eames, "Library Guides: Who We Are: LGBTQ+ Americans," University Libraries, University of Washington, February 8, 2018, https://guides.lib.uw.edu/research/whoweare/LGBTQamericans.

Bibliography

Eames, L. E. "Library Guides: Who We Are: African Americans." University Libraries. University of Washington, February 8, 2018. https://guides.lib.uw.edu/research/whoweare/AfricanAmericans.
———. "Library Guides: Who We Are: Asian Americans and Pacific Islanders." University Libraries. University of Washington, February 8, 2018. https://guides.lib.uw.edu/research/whoweare/AAPI.
———. "Library Guides: Who We Are: Diversity in Government Documents: Home." University Libraries. University of Washington, February 8, 2018. https://guides.lib.uw.edu/research/whoweare/home.
———. "Library Guides: Who We Are: Jewish Americans." University Libraries. University of Washington, February 8, 2018. https://guides.lib.uw.edu/research/whoweare/JewishAmericans.

———. "Library Guides: Who We Are: Latinx Americans." University Libraries. University of Washington, February 8, 2018. https://guides.lib.uw.edu/research/whoweare/LatinxAmericans.

———. "Library Guides: Who We Are: LGBTQ+ Americans." University Libraries. University of Washington, February 8, 2018. https://guides.lib.uw.edu/research/whoweare/LGBTQamericans.

———. "Library Guides: Who We Are: Muslim Americans." University Libraries. University of Washington, February 8, 2018. https://guides.lib.uw.edu/research/whoweare/MuslimAmericans.

———. "Library Guides: Who We Are: Women." University Libraries. University of Washington, February 8, 2018. https://guides.lib.uw.edu/research/whoweare/WomenInAmerica

Chapter 7

Call and Response:

Delicate Conversations in Collection Development

Alexis L. Pavenick

She is passionate about collection development practices that are inclusive, representative, and reflective of the diversity and commonality of her campus and of human experience.

She has learned and continues to seek a wide breadth of knowledge in the humanities and social sciences, web and interactive media design/development, instructional design, and online classroom instruction.

Seven months into my new full-time librarian position, my collections development officer offered me the wonderful if challenging task of managing a large endowment fund. I said yes to it before I understood its parameters. That conversation went something like this:

> "Do you want to take over the Schwab Endowment in your collections development?"
> "Sure!" I immediately replied, being new and helpful. "What does that entail?"

"Well, the money comes through sporadically and it needs to be spent rather quickly. It doesn't roll over."
"OK, so—."
"The content is mainly Gay novels, poetry, and biography."
"Cool! So—."
"The current installment for this round is $22,000."
I paused in my auto-response, pushing the phone painfully closer to my ear, "I'm sorry, just to clarify, twenty-two *thousand* dollars."
"Yes. You've got two months. Thanks so much for doing this!"
Well, OK. OK! After taking several long breaths, I went to see my co-worker, who had just been released from this mammoth assignment. He opened his door to smile broadly at me, "It's great that you took on Schwab! I'll give you all my spreadsheets. Don't stress about it. It's OK if you don't spend all the money."

And I knew at that moment, I would spend all of the money. Oh yes… yes, I would.

Back in my office, looking over the mission statement of the endowment in relation to the spreadsheet of past purchases, I saw the issue at stake. The statement was beautifully direct:

> In 1995 Arnold T. Schwab, CSULB Professor Emeritus of English, established a named endowment for the purchase of books, especially poetry and fiction, with gay themes—particularly those books issued by gay, non-mainstream, or chapbook publishers. The endowment also supports the purchase of biographies or critical studies of gay poets or novelists.

The majority of these items would be standard paperback books, with price tags that rarely ranged above $30 each. Even with the impetus to go "hog wild" and buy every gay-themed piece of literature or biography of the moment I could find, it would be hard to spend tens of thousands of dollars every eighteen months. I also felt the collection deserved more thoughtful development.

Specifically, I was interested in the phrase "non-mainstream." It occurred to me that the term had a potentially much wider meaning than it may have in

1995. That was when the *first* light bulb lit up in my mind. I called my collections development officer and, in my most friendly East Coast-influenced tone, I started, "Let me ask you this: How are we defining 'gay' and 'non-mainstream'?"

"Gay in this instance likely means male homosexuality. Non-mainstream is …well, it could be a lot of things. Why?"

"I'm wondering if we can select LGBTQIA+ themes under that umbrella. Including Gender Theory?"

"OK—"

"And any subject, like in the social or formal sciences, as well as the humanities?"

"OK—"

"And include authors who identify as LGBTQIA+, even if their text doesn't have LGBTQIA+ content?"

"Is that all?"

I thought about it. "Yes."

The request was approved.

Then, my *second* light bulb sparked: I needed help—and a lot of it. So, I did something new for my library: I asked for assistance—from across the campus.

Storytelling Goal

To entice and encourage faculty, students, and librarians to be engaged with suggesting items for a collection.

Audience

Faculty, students, and librarians who would like to contribute collection development ideas.

Steps to Research: Faculty and Librarians

First, I sent out an email to my library colleagues asking them for two things: (1) to send me their own wish list for Schwab, and (2) to forward an email request to their faculty liaisons in all disciplines. The email to forward was brief and succinct in its request and indicated I was the direct contact. (See Practical Examples below.) I asked for every possible LGBTQIA+-related text people had been keeping in their notes and wish lists.

The response was glorious. Suggestions came in from my colleague librarians, my own faculty in my subject specialties, and, thanks to the forwarded emails, from faculty in women's, gender and sexuality studies, anthropology, sociology, environmental science, the French, German, Italian, Spanish, and Russian language departments, linguistics, and children's literature, with a huge addition by our children's literature librarian, who had a wish list a mile long.

Naturally, these faculty requests were easy to vet. I researched the titles and they all fit Schwab and our larger library mission profile. This was expected, as these suggestions were generally items professors had wanted to see in the stacks but did not prioritize because of smaller budgets.

The bigger task with the faculty was the additional step of searching our catalog to see if we already owned the items. It is my experience that people will not always look to see if we have something before suggesting we should buy it. Yet, I didn't want to discourage people from sending me ideas by asking them to check the stacks, so I did not amend my request. Happily, in my case, we have a federated OneSearch and can easily search by ISBN, so the process went smoothly.

I did also politely list items we already had in our collection, with call numbers, in my thank you reply.

Steps to Research: Students

When the faculty sent the request out to their students, my email responses became a little more formal. Student suggestions were often more popular in content, thereby often less literarily or academically acclaimed. One example is *50 Queers Who Changed the World: A Celebration of LGBTQIA+ Icons*.[1] This is a lovely, colorful book with very short biographies made to entice readers to do further research on their own. In dealing with such suggestions, my main interest was to verify the item had truthful if basic information. If it did, I purchased it for its approachability. In cases of literature, such as a novel or a biography, I typically purchased it if it had positive reviews from CHOICE and LGBTQIA+ review sources like the Lambda Literary Awards, Stonewall Book Awards, and the American Library Association Rainbow Round Table.

Yet, I also purchased items that had rave reviews on Amazon. Some popular romance novels were high on the student suggestion list, so I included a variety of those and one full-length series. These choices were part of a balance to satisfy requests while still seeking to preference materials that may be used academically, rather than as recreational reading. If I worked at a public library or some other style of institution, my preferences would be in line with those mission statements.

On this first occasion of managing the Schwab endowment, I only had one set of suggestions that gave me pause, and what I determined to do in that instance is now an approach that I continue. This is where the story gets delicate.

As I had asked faculty to get student suggestions as well, an anthropology professor gave my request as a project for some LGBTQIA+ students with whom he worked. Led by a non-gender identifying student, over the course of a month the group compiled a list of more than eighty items. They considered suggestions from CSULB students, course syllabi, and community members. The items were categorized and included detailed explanations and rationale. They even included a definition of a zine, in case I was not aware (I am, but I really appreciated this level of interest.) I could not have asked for a more thorough and apt set of suggestions.

Ninety-nine percent of what they recommended was an easy vet and purchase. When I got to their "sexualities" section, however, I had to stop and think over this particular title, published in 1997: *Leathersex: A Guide for the Curious Outsider and the Serious Player* by Joseph W. Bean.[2]

The students had done their homework. Joseph W. Bean is an important figure in the gay bondage scene and its related communities in the US, and *Leathersex* is a popular book in its genre. I knew this book was akin in purpose to sexual self-care texts we already offered, such as *The Joy of Sex* and similar texts for same-sex partners. Yet, as I researched its content through methods such as Amazon's "look inside" feature, the explicit nature of the book's tone and approach made me wonder if this item fit into our general profile. I was concerned that Bean's casual approach to describing physically and emotionally challenging sexual intimacy might be taken less seriously if compared to our other, more formal sex instruction books. Would the difference in tone intimate to patrons that a person had to be rather ribald and expressive to participate in the BDSM (bondage, discipline, dominance/submission, sadism/masochism) and fetish communities? More research was necessary. This was my research question: Was there a text that explored the same content, with less cultural scene jargon and jocose commentary? For the record, my concern over this particular title took the most time of all the suggestions I examined, yet it still only amounted to the better part of two workdays.

My research yielded a greater understanding and appreciation of how all of the students' suggested authors in their area of "sexualities" were socially related to each other. The group had also suggested *The Lesbian S/M Safety Manual*[3] and *The New Topping*.[4] These I was able to find as electronic texts, and in looking them all up, I discovered the authors were connected through being in a cultural scene at the same or overlapping times. This led me to discover that Bean had contributed to a text written by Guy Baldwin, *Ties that Bind*.[5] Baldwin's text presents selected articles from two important periodicals in this community: *Drummer* and *Ties that Bind*. Baldwin, also a licensed therapist and prominent in the BDSM community, gives soberly worded context to the magazine content, showing two sides of presentation. This seemed to me an effective compromise for our collection.

So, I had found a substitution I thought would work. All I had left to do was explain it to the students and get their feedback. Some librarians might ask, why bother to tell them? It's just a list of suggestions. My answer to this question is the crux of my collection development approach: I want to engage my patrons and I want them to do the main work of investigation for me. In exchange, I want them to know I have looked over each suggestion with care and I have selected what I believe are items appropriate for the collection. In tandem, I want them to know why I do not choose something and what I can offer in place of it. This helps them to better understand what I'm looking for and shows that I am very willing to find middle ground.

In my email thank you to the leader of the student group, I detailed which items we already had, with call numbers. I noted the available links to the books I was able to find free online, and, finally, I offered Baldwin's text in place of Bean's with this phrasing, edited here for clarification out of context:

> With regard to the titles you have suggested under "sexualities," it is important to keep in mind that we are primarily a research library, so our purview is not directly focused on self-care. This does not prevent access, as patrons may request the loan of any item through our interlibrary loan system.
>
> That said, I agree that texts addressing all types of sexual instruction are important additions to our collection. To keep with the theme of your suggested BDSM texts, outside of the electronically accessible items, I will purchase the following title: *Ties That Bind: SM / Leather / Fetish / Erotic Style: Issues, Commentaries and Advice* (2003) by Guy Baldwin, ISBN 978-1881943099.

It's useful to know that I stressed over this part and had a much longer draft with all of my explanations. In discussing it with my co-workers, however, they suggested that I accept the fact that at the end of the day, I'm in charge of the collection, and I made no promises to purchase in my request for suggestions. Still, it helped a great deal that my university has a robust interlibrary loan service and also would have allowed for the purchase if I had decided in favor of Bean's book. If these two elements were not the case, I likely would have sent the longer version of my email reply with my thoughts and explanations. I was also quite ready to have a full and frank discussion with the students in person.

Yet, the students approved my choice and their leader responded with heartfelt thanks that I had taken the time to do the research. I was very relieved and satisfied with the compromise.

Take-aways

The lesson of this story is what so many librarians already know and believe, that inclusion and diversity can and should be represented in our collections. But when we make a big call for help, perhaps a campus-wide call such as I did, the instances of dealing with suggestions that may be outside our experience or comfort zone can, and likely will, increase. Such collection development stories remind us that inclusion *includes us*. Showing we support our patron community through patient research, time management, and sincere communication really can work successfully.

The practical lesson of my experience is that engaging with faculty and students about collection development gets the librarian involved in what is happening intellectually, academically, socially, and culturally in the research and reading interests of the campus. The wider we cast our net, the more we see the interconnectedness of content. Facilitation comes down to being friendly and having strong time management.

I am fully aware that I am privileged to manage the Schwab endowment and lucky that it is a big sum of money addressing a big topic. But what I learned from this experience translated to my smaller budgets and specific collection themes. I now habitually reach out, collect ideas, keep files, and manage my time to include this work as part of my day, not a crush at the beginning or end of the semester. The engagement creates connections with faculty and students such that now, when I walk across campus, people from all manner of disciplines recognize me and stop to say hello. This makes my work easier, more productive, and much more rewarding.

Delivery

There are a few methods of delivery for the story about your collection. To begin, reach out to faculty and students you already have good relations with to get their ideas for the collection and to get further ideas about other people who may be interested in making suggestions. From there, ask your fellow library faculty to forward your invitation to their liaisons and others whom they think might want to contribute. Finally, branch out to entice faculty and students to contribute suggestions for your collection by presenting at faculty meetings, clubs, dormitories, and content-related events.

If a Suggestion Does Not Fit with Your Collection's Mission

Take a moment to consider informal ways of better describing your mission to the person who made the suggestion. Also, do a little research to see if another text or item may have similar content that more closely aligns with your collection's vision. Offer this information and alternatives to the person. Be open to discussion about it.

This approach may accomplish three things: (1) the person may appreciate that you have taken their request seriously, (2) the person may garner a better understanding of what the collection is about, and (3) you will have learned something you didn't know before about the topic.

Theory

Collection development may feel limited when only librarian research and the voices of some key interested people (often faculty) are included. On the other hand, opening your collection development to a wide variety of people can also be intimidating because you may invite suggestions for materials you do not wish to include in your purchases.

My story shows one way to manage that concern. The plot of my story is about reaching out, listening, and managing time to respond with enthusiasm and kindness to collection suggestions. Through a bit of extra time in research and finding alternative suggestions, it is possible that everyone can agree to an item, and thus the collection is expanded with awareness and inclusion.

As well, the storytelling itself is a way to encourage people to think about collections and how they may be developed. Many people do not know how collections are built or what responsibilities a librarian takes on in terms of budget and distribution. Knowing the story of your collection and inviting others to join in its growth can naturally increase interest, understanding, and usage, and these are key development goals.

Cultural Considerations

It is vital that your collection reflects the needs and interests of your library patrons. However, limited budgets and even conventional mission statements may not entirely support that goal. Those of us who are given the job of collection development can benefit our populations by reaching out to them to learn what they want to see in their library. While it is our job to keep a balance between our budget and what the institution requires in our collection choices, this does not prevent us from being knowledgeable about what exists in the world, regardless of whether we have it in our collection. Being aware of the material and where it can be found is a skill anyone who manages collections can develop and use daily, whether or not budgets or mission statements support inclusive growth.

How to Manage Time Vetting Suggestions

- Collect suggestions in one place, such as an email folder or a desktop folder.
- Reply in thanks immediately to each suggestion with a note that you will be back in touch to confirm what has been chosen.
- Mark or organize the suggestion by the date it was received.
- Allot one hour a day, or three to five hours a week, to research the suggestions and reply to the contributor with your choices.
- Try to get back with patrons within two weeks.

Timely, enthusiastic replies foster communication, goodwill, and future suggestions from the contributor and those they may encourage to contact you.

Vetting the suggestion does not need to take very long at all. Finding the item online via a commercial bookseller or in a library catalog will give you basic information about its content, and this is typically enough to decide.

Blogs and particular review boards also help. Also, search WorldCat to see what other libraries may hold the item. Looking at WorldCat has two benefits: first, you can consider what other libraries have chosen the item for their collection; second, if you choose *not* to select the item for your collection, you can then suggest where patrons may go to find it and/or determine if it is available through your interlibrary loan service if you have one.

Leave the difficult searches to when you can schedule more time. When I initially reviewed the content of Bean's book, I knew I would need more time to learn about it before making a decision. I marked time on my calendar to really investigate it and to look for potential alternatives. I kept the contributors informed of my timeline, and that created a good connection. Their suggestions did not go into a vacuum. I was regularly engaged with them as part of the collection development process.

Practical Examples

My email request for help, sent to my librarian colleagues and my own department liaisons; this email is phrased so that it can be forwarded:

> Hello Everyone,
>
> The generous Arnold T. Schwab Endowment has funds available for one-time purchases of LGBTQIA+ items in all disciplines. I would like your help identifying resources.
>
> I am hoping that you might look to your own wish lists and ask other faculty if they have any items that fall under the LGBTQIA+ purview that they would like us to have in the collections. All areas of study will be considered; the content and/or author should be related to LGBTQIA+ topics and interests.
>
> People who would like to offer suggestions can email me directly. I just need authors/titles, but if suggestions come with ISBNs or links, they are much appreciated!

Cheers and Best!
Alexis
(Followed by my contact information)

Email note when an item suggested is already in the stacks:

Happy News! I found that we already have two of your suggestions in the stacks! Here are their Call Numbers…

Endnotes

1. Dan Jones and Michèle Rosenthal, *50 Queers Who Changed the World: A Celebration of LGBTQ Icons* (Richmond, AU: Hardie Grant Books, 2017).
2. Joseph W. Bean, *Leathersex: A Guide for the Curious Outsider and the Serious Player*, 2nd ed. (Sawtry, UK: Daedalus Pub. Co., 1997).
3. Pat Califia, ed., *The Lesbian S/M Safety Manual* (New York: Alyson Books, 1988).
4. Dossie Easton and Janet W. Hardy. *The New Topping* (Emeryville, CA: Greenery Press, 2002).
5. Guy Baldwin, *Ties That Bind: The SM/Leather/Fetish Erotic Style: Issues, Commentaries, and Advice*, 2nd ed. (Sawtry, UK: Daedalus Pub. Co., 2003).

Bibliography

American Library Association's Gay, Lesbian, Bisexual, and Transgender Round Table. Accessed July 1, 2020. http://ala.org/rt/rrt.
———. "Stonewall Book Awards List." Accessed July 1, 2020. http://ala.org/rt/rrt/award/stonewall/honored.
Baldwin, Guy. *Ties That Bind: The SM/Leather/Fetish Erotic Style: Issues, Commentaries, and Advice*. 2nd ed. Sawtry, UK: Daedalus Pub. Co., 2003.
Bean, Joseph W. *Leathersex: A Guide for the Curious Outsider and the Serious Player*. 2nd ed. Sawtry, UK: Daedalus Pub. Co., 1997.
Califia, Pat, ed. *The Lesbian S/M Safety Manual*. New York: Alyson Books, 1988.
California State University. "Arnold T. Schwab Endowment Collection." University Library, Long Beach. Accessed July 1, 2020. http://csulb.libguides.com/schwabcollection.
Easton, Dossie, and Janet W. Hardy. *The New Topping*. Emeryville, CA: Greenery Press, 2002.
Jones, Dan, and Michèle Rosenthal. *50 Queers Who Changed the World: A Celebration of LGBTQ Icons*. Richmond, AU: Hardie Grant Books, 2017.
Lambda Literary Awards. "Lambda Literary Awards Finalists & Winners." Accessed July 1, 2020. http://lambdaliterary.org/previous-winners-2/.

Chapter 8

Choose Your Own Path:

Using Primary Sources and Oral History Interviews to Promote Life Experiences Found in Special Collections and University Archives

Harrison Wick

Since 2002, he has worked as an archivist for academic libraries and historical societies. The first large-scale project he completed was processing the congressional papers of United States Senator William V. Roth, Jr., who created the Roth IRA, for the Delaware Historical Society. For three years, he was the archivist for Misericordia University in Dallas, Pennsylvania. During this time, he started writing and presenting about Pennsylvania's regional history. Dr. Wick's scholarship includes publications and grant research into industrial history, military leadership, and the history of higher education. Since joining the IUP Libraries in 2007, he has collaborated with colleagues to curate several University Museum exhibits that have publicized archival and museum collections, including coal culture, artwork, and literature. Dr.

Wick is also interested in reformatting audio/visual recordings and providing digital access to primary sources.

Storytelling and oral history traditions are an important part of the human experience that dates back to ancient times. These types of primary source materials are available in many historical repositories, including archives, libraries, museums, and history centers, and can be interpreted in many different ways. Researchers and professional historians value the importance of recording oral history interviews. Generations of people from all walks of life have heard stories told about their families and the origins of different groups of people. These stories document geographic relocation, including immigration, military service, personal history, and socio-economic upheaval during uncertain times, which are just as relevant today as they were more than a century ago.

These stories and primary sources are unique to every individual and relevant to today's society, reflecting historical events on a personal level. Primary sources document historical events of the last century, and it is important to teach the values of storytelling and documenting modern events such as COVID-19 to students. These experiences have dramatically changed cultural landscapes, and it is important for educators to recognize the importance of oral history interviews and how students can learn to share a good story.

In marketing special collections as a resource within libraries, it is important to discuss resources about the stories of people's lives, including written primary sources and oral history interviews. As a librarian, my marketing and outreach presentations promote special collections by using proactive storytelling techniques to discuss societal changes and incorporate different types of sources through discussion, visual resources, and hands-on activities with books, photographs, and documents. The promotion of these resources has led to collection development opportunities, including collaborative exhibits and multidisciplinary presentations. The primary sources available for use in IUP Special Collections and Archives reflect diverse cultures, cross-sections of society, and generational histories.

Storytelling Goal

To introduce students and teachers to methods of utilizing the different types of primary sources available to the public and to demonstrate how these resources from archival repositories and academic libraries can be used in instruction. Methods of instruction using primary sources are varied, but in most cases, instruction included credited courses, one-shot bibliographic instruction sessions, or scheduled appointments with students and their professors. There are many types of primary sources that students can choose from to write about the personal experiences of individuals and add historical context from their own research. Using primary sources, including oral history interviews, photographs, scrapbooks, and theater programs, provides students ample opportunity to learn about the history of the theater department.

Audience

Many undergraduate and graduate students participate in bibliographic instruction sessions who are not familiar with using library resources or primary sources. Students visiting Special Collections and University Archives may or may not have experience conducting research with primary sources such as archival collections and oral history interviews in their research projects.[1] Participating courses may include students majoring in history, anthropology, geography, labor relations, theater, and fine arts. However, bibliographic instruction sessions utilizing primary sources has also included community members, faculty, visiting researchers, and alumni from a variety of departments.

Delivery

During an in-person or virtual bibliographic instruction session in Special Collections and University Archives, students are taught about primary sources found in archival collections that were donated by individuals either associated with an institution or specific geographic region. Bibliographic instruction offers opportunities for students and faculty to learn about library resources that can be specific to their research. These types of documents can include correspondence and documents (handwritten and printed), memorabilia, diaries or journals, oral history interviews, photographs, and scrapbooks. Many of these resources can be digitized to make it more convenient for students, faculty, and researchers to utilize diverse collections.

Depending on the number of students in each class, each student may be able to work with an individual collection. If the class size is larger, small groups of students can work together on a single archival collection. During a fifty- or sixty-minute period, this type of exercise gives the students twenty to twenty-five minutes to evaluate the collection-finding aid document, look at specific primary sources in the archival collection, and report or present their findings as part of the exercise during the bibliographic instruction session. Librarians and archivists often customize bibliographic instruction sessions that are designed to discuss specific resources requested by faculty for student assignments.

Theory

By reading and examining the different types of primary sources and personal accounts that are available in archival collections, students will learn about and empathize with the experiences written by others. Special Collections and University Archives contain many different primary sources that will help students learn more about history.[2] Students use available documents, audio/visual recordings, photographs, and other types of primary sources to learn about the daily lives and events people experienced while living in different regions. Oral history interviews provide students a unique opportunity to listen to people from an earlier generation. Many archival collections reflect significant and historical events throughout history, and students will learn about experiences from previous generations.[3] Students will have the opportunity to work with primary sources that were created by individuals who were perhaps close to their age and came from a similar background or geographic region.

Cultural Considerations

Archival collections include donations from people who have come from all walks of life. The primary sources available in historical repositories, including Special Collections and University Archives, represent diverse viewpoints from many different cultures, gender identity, ethnicities, and socio-economic backgrounds.[4] Different types of primary sources donated by alumni, employees, and the community may include documents, interviews, photographs, audio/visual recordings, and scrapbooks. The use of these types of primary sources can be significant and thought-provoking in a way that will help undergraduate and graduate students, as well as first-generation college students better understand history and how to reflect on using primary sources in their research.

Based on the course or assignment, faculty may select the types of archival resources that students can use in their research, or students may identify a collection they would like to consult as either a group or individually. These types of projects may include transcriptions of handwritten documents, comparative analysis, or historical research, which are important for students to learn about and be aware of the cultural lenses that may be an integral part of primary sources from people of different and diverse backgrounds. By having the opportunity to interpret oral history interviews and other types of primary sources, students will have the opportunity to learn about diversity and inclusion.

Practical Example

In preparation for the fortieth anniversary of the theater department, a professor from the College of Fine Arts contacted the IUP Special Collections and University Archives to ask if students could participate in a project to interview alumni and faculty and help identify photographs associated with theater productions at Indiana University of Pennsylvania. According to one author, "What could be more transformative for the field of art history than empowering students to seek their own answers, through the critical and creative reading of primary evidence."[5] Utilizing primary sources, including photographs, scrapbooks, and theater programs, the special collections librarian and university archivist contacted several alumni and retired faculty to participate in this collaborative project. After receiving bibliographic instruction on how to identify photographs and use archival materials, undergraduate students interviewed groups of alumni and retired faculty from the theater department. Participating students learned about the forty-year history of the department and more than a century of theater productions on campus. Students also learned about archival techniques to conduct oral history interviews and how to properly identify photographs and negatives of theater productions. This successful project led to future opportunities for students, alumni, teachers, and librarians to collect primary sources.

This was a two-part project that included students visiting the IUP Special Collections and University Archives to receive bibliographic instruction, a site visit to the College of Fine Arts to see new archival materials, and the opportunity for students to interview alumni. Students were given instruction on how to conduct interviews, examine primary sources, and identify archival materials. This bibliographic instruction session and collaboration was extremely popular with participating theater alumni, current students, as well as current and retired faculty. These groups were brought together in a new way that encouraged further cooperation. This project led to the recording of oral history interviews that discussed past performances and the forty-year history of the theater department. This collaborative project was beneficial to marketing the services and resources provided by the IUP Special Collections and University Archives.

There is a great deal of potential in teaching students how to use and incorporate primary sources found in archival and historical repositories into their research. Bibliographic instruction sessions can include library services and methods of conducting research and how to find, handle, and interpret archival resources from different time periods and cultural perspectives. Integrating primary sources into bibliographic instruction can offer students access to a variety of archival collections that can be integrated into research projects and course assignments. One of the most significant challenges to using primary sources in research and bibliographic instruction is handling and repeated use. Paper-based documents may be printed or written on acidic and embrittled paper, and audio/visual recordings can become obsolete over time.

Digitization can be an important tool in improving and providing access to fragile primary sources. Many paper-based original documents and audio/visual recordings can be damaged through repeated use, including handling during research, digitization, or reformatting. Technological obsolesce or media failure are genuine concerns that can irrevocably damage audio/visual recordings when using or digitizing formats, including reel-to-reel, audio cassette, or video cassette tape. The conversion of these outdated media formats is essential to prevent irrevocable data loss. Providing access to an oral history interview in a digital format is much more convenient for researchers.[6] Students need access to primary sources that may be unique or only available in a fragile, outdated format. In many cases, resources can be digitized and accessed in a digital format through an institutional repository.

Endnotes

1. Michelle McCoy, "The Manuscript as Question: Teaching Primary Sources in the Archives—The China Missions Project," *College & Research Libraries* 71, no. 1 (2010): 54.
2. McCoy, "The Manuscript as Question," 60.
3. Ella Holmes, "Building Engaging Teaching Materials with Primary Sources," *Agora* 50, no. 1 (June 2015): 62.
4. Rachel M. Grove Rohrbaugh, "Teaching with Primary Sources," *The American Archivist* 80, no. 2 (Fall/Winter 2017): 465.
5. Liza Kirwin, "Teaching with Primary Sources," introduction to In the Round, *Panorama: Journal of the Association of Historians of American Art* 5, no. 2 (Fall 2019): 1.
6. Rohrbaugh, "Teaching with Primary Sources," 465.

Bibliography

Holmes, Ella. "Building Engaging Teaching Materials with Primary Sources." *Agora* 50, no. 1 (June 2015): 62–66. https://search.informit.org/doi/10.3316/ielapa.431841872295774.

Kirwin, Liza. "Teaching with Primary Sources." Introduction to In the Round, *Panorama: Journal of the Association of Historians of American Art* 5, no. 2 (Fall 2019): 1–3. https://doi.org/10.24926/24716839.2298.

McCoy, Michelle. "The Manuscript as Question: Teaching Primary Sources in the Archives—The China Missions Project." *College & Research Libraries* 71, no 1 (2010): 49–62. https://doi.org/10.5860/0710049.

Rohrbaugh, Rachel M. Grove. "Teaching with Primary Sources." *The American Archivist* 80, no. 2 (Fall/Winter 2017): 462–66. https://doi.org/10.17723/0360-9081-80.2.462.

Chapter 9

Let's Tell a Story:
Narrative, Constructivism, and Accessibility

Anders Tobiason

I started making video tutorials as a graduate student in library and information science, took a few years off, and started again as a reference librarian at Portland State University. While I always had a sense that video tutorials could be better than they often are, I wasn't really sure exactly what that meant—that is, until I went to remake a few older videos to reflect some changes in the library catalog. How could I communicate those changes in a way that was engaging and helped move the viewer through the video? Then I remembered an old lesson from teaching music theory: tell them a story. For me, telling a story was a foundational aspect of both writing and teaching. So, I thought I would try it out. I was going to tell stories in my videos!

Thinking back to those days teaching music theory also reminded me to focus on accessibility. I taught a student who was blind for two semesters, and the lessons they imparted to me have informed my teaching practice ever since. A really important one was that following how to do a task was so much easier if the story surrounding it was engaging and included direct causal relationships. This was a nascent version of the idea of creating a breadcrumb trail for students to follow in learning a particular concept. Indeed, this whole process of thinking through creating better and more accessible videos is like following a trail of breadcrumbs. Each connection back to classroom teaching and engaging with the specifics of the particular

123

videos I was remaking led me further and further toward understanding narrative as an accessibility tool. It is still a work in progress, as all good journeys are, but the trail is certainly one I enjoy exploring.

Storytelling Goal

I decided to use storytelling/narrative over other techniques because it allows viewers to follow along with the story and use the story's causal links to form concrete memory-based connections. It also allows for enhanced accessibility by describing both how to do something, and what the consequences of the doing are, and why they are important. Just describing in detail is vital, of course, but adding in storytelling creates those concrete moments of causality.

In addition, I turned to narrative as a means to create a "trail of breadcrumbs" effect so that all users can follow the content. By grounding video tutorial design in both Universal Design for Learning as well as narrative teaching strategies, we can work to create truly accessible and engaging videos. Instead of just illustrating a concept, the idea of telling a story allows for us as creators to connect with how we teach, rather than just what we teach. Using narrative fundamentally entails inviting the viewer/listener to participate in the task, rather than just passively receive the information.

Audience

The video is intended for anyone who interacts with the Ex Libris PRIMO ILS system, not just Portland State Students, though it is branded for PSU.

Delivery

The video is hosted on the Portland State University (PSU) Library YouTube page. It is embedded in many course and subject guides as well as directly in the PSU Course Management system for certain classes. It is used to instruct students about the ways they can use persistent limiters and filters to enhance their research process. It is one of a number of short videos that librarians can use in place of, or in conjunction with, in-person interactions should they need or want to do so.

Theory

Narrative and/or storytelling has a long history in educational theory and is generally considered to be part of the constructivist school of teaching and learning.[1] In constructivism, learners actively connect concepts and are invited to recreate learning experiences on their own.[2] By using narrative and storytelling techniques, we invite the student/learner along with us in the mode of discovery. Narrative is a form of storytelling that makes use of causality and direct communication to engage the reader/listener in a story. The key to narrative is a description of what happens during and as a result of an action rather than a static description of the thing itself.[3]

Constructivism is, by its nature, a storytelling process, whether in creating narratives that allow for students to experience a particular concept in terms of their own lived experience or encouraging students to work alongside the teacher by inviting them to actively do so. In other words, we construct an educational experience that is active and student-centered. As Linda Harasim writes, "Guided by the teacher, students actively construct their knowledge rather than mechanically ingest knowledge from the teacher or the textbook. The teacher thus plays an active and essential role, assisting in identifying a knowledge problem, providing guidance in how to understand it and suggesting resources."[4] The idea of a teacher as a guide is particularly prescient here. What is one of the main functions of a guide? It is not just to move people through a space but also to tell a story of that space in order to empower others to interact with it in their own ways. Indeed, Harasim also writes that "constructivism seeks to tap into and trigger the student's innate curiosity about the world and how things work. Students are not expected to reinvent the wheel but to attempt to understand how it turns, how it functions."[5] Using narrative in this context allows all students, both disabled and abled, to understand how the wheel turns rather than having to reinvent it for themselves.

With this understanding of how storytelling can be constructed to enhance student learning and accessibility, let's take a look at the script for a video I created and see how it plays out. The title of the video is "Persistent Filters and Limiters."[6] Stories always begin with a problem or stressor that needs some attention. In the video, the problem, as it were, is having to refilter search results every time one changes a keyword or does a new search. A potential way to alleviate this stress is to use the lock filter tool. We can imagine a story starting to form from these basic elements. The narrator begins by stating that "one of the more frustrating things when searching within our library catalog used to be that every time you changed a search term and redid a search, all of the filters and limiters you were using got reset as well. Well, that is no longer the case. You can now lock any limiter or filter that you are using in one search to be used in the entire searching session."[7] Not only is this statement the beginning of a story, but it also actively constructs a situation a researcher will be familiar with and can then add their narratives and experiences to.

The next section of the video invites the user to do a series of tasks alongside the narrator. This doing-alongside-the-teacher style of interaction is another hallmark of constructionism.[8] During this series of tasks, the narrator tells a story about why doing these tasks is important and makes the causal relationships between the tasks clear. The description of the tasks is also spelled out in detail to make sure that the story can be followed easily. This clarity also engages the user by explicitly describing how each filter functions. In fact, the end of this section directly asks the user a question: "Are they exactly on the topic we were looking for or do we need to change or add to our keywords?"[9] Here we find another moment where active participation in the learning process is constructed. And it is also a crucial storytelling element. The statement asks the viewer to place themselves in the story by evaluating this results list. This, then, is a concrete version of the frustration mentioned at the beginning of the video: the user may find the results list lacking and need to redo the search but will be frustrated when the filters reset as well. So now, to alleviate some of this frustration; "It's time to lock the filters and show why it may be a path forward." This is the meta-story, but within each description of the tasks, there are also discrete storytelling elements that create causal connections. For instance, the video describes how to lock the filters, add a new keyword to the search box, and finally run the search. But it is not enough just to describe the task—that is not a story; rather, the key here is that the video details the effect of doing the tasks in this order. In other words, selecting the lock filter tool before changing a keyword keeps the filters locked when running a new search. As the narrator states, "The filters stayed with us as we changed our search terms. Awesome!"[10]

The video continues to mirror Harasim's concept of the teacher as a guide by describing other ways that the locking filters tool can help alleviate research stress. In the process, it allows space for the creation of more connections between using the tool and individual lived experience. The final section of the video provides a concrete example of the larger effects of locking the filters by ruminating on a little bit of an expanded research technique. "You can have multiple searches in different tabs and keep some or all of the limiters the same."[11] This is an example that researchers may encounter in real life and, by describing the causal effect between locking the filter and having multiple searches, the narrator pushes the story forward again. As is true of the video as a whole, the user is invited in to tell their own version of the story based on individual experiences. Thus, the story grows the idea that using the tool can alleviate some research stress though, perhaps, in unexpected ways.

The video ends by stating that "locking filters and limiters can help you efficiently search for resources by eliminating the need to re-filter every time you search!"[12] The key word here is "can." Instead of saying that the tool absolutely *does* make research more efficient (which is a highly problematic and charged concept anyway), the video allows the researcher to make that judgment call for themselves. The story delineates the causal connections that show why the tool may be helpful but in the end does not prescribe absolute meaning to it. By using the techniques of storytelling, both in the long form of the entire video and the short form of individual sentences, coupled with a consciousness that it is part of a constructionist school of teaching, we can create space for users to interact with a tool on their own and tell their own stories of its usefulness. This, in turn, can create more accessible learning objects. As Carlos Leon writes, "Producing narratives is not only an ability that is more or less natural, but a specific topology for storing information."[13] He then further clarifies the idea of narratives as creating information storage containers by stating that "narrative objects are then created. Full narratives are then created from these narrative objects as constituents. Finally, narratives are the main elements of the narrative-aware episodic memory and procedural-semantic memory."[14] As we shall see in the next section, creating a semantic structure is a key feature of accessibility.

Cultural Considerations

One of the main goals of web accessibility is to create clear paths to and through web-based resources and web pages. WCAG 2.1.3 directly addresses this idea by giving specific guidelines, such as "instructions provided for understanding and operating content do not rely solely on sensory characteristics of components such as shape, color, size, visual location, orientation, or sound."[15] The rest of that section of WCAG also addresses these concerns.[16] In general, one of the basic ideas here can be described as a trail of breadcrumbs. We often think of web accessibility as making the visual-based nature of web resources into something that can be understood aurally. This is where intention, causality, and sequence (in other words, narrative) come into play—both narrative on the local sentence level but also a narrative structure in the entire short video.

When we think about web accessibility, one of the main tenants is to create a semantic structure or a logical document structure. Semantic structure means creating logical connections and steps between different pages or parts of a webpage on the backend or code side.[17] If we take this basic principle and sit with it for a bit, it starts to sound a lot like narrative. In other words, what makes semantic structure so compelling from an accessibility standpoint are the causal connections between pages and objects that allow for any user, whether disabled or not, to access them without major difficulties. Making this explicit when we are talking or explaining a concept in a video, therefore, follows this tenant of web accessibility.

Web accessibility is not just for people with disabilities. It, in fact, benefits us all by using concrete planned structures to guide us through the webspace. By making logical and causal connections between elements that are linked in webspace, a basic sense of flow is achieved. And narrative, in the sense of an active description of a series of causally connected events, can also be said to have a basic sense of flow as an underlying goal. Thus, when creating a video, using narrative elements assists in constructing an accessible learning experience. While this certainly benefits differently abled users, it is not exclusively for them. For students who have any library or research anxiety, using narrative builds a structure that they can latch on to. Just as with web accessibility more generally, using the causal and logical connections inherent in storytelling allows us to create videos that guide students through a process or concept.

Practical Example

Persistent Filters and Limiters (https://www.youtube.com/watch?v=6ci8U_KYtfM):[18]

Script:

Doing research is often a time-consuming and tedious process, so we at the library keep looking for ways that we can make the process a little less so.

One of the more frustrating things when searching within our library catalog used to be that every time you changed a search term and redid a search, all of the filters and limiters you were using got reset as well.

Well, that is no longer the case.

You can now lock any limiter or filter that you are using in one search to be used in the entire searching session.

So, let's take a look at how to keep those filters across multiple searches.

Begin by signing in to the library catalog, always a good idea for accessing resources. Then, type in some keywords, for instance, "electric vehicle", into the general library search box and press enter or the search button.

Start by limiting the results to the past 10 years by typing 2009 into the date limiter under the refine my results header. And pressing Refine.

Then, under the header availability, select the Peer Reviewed Journals filter.

And since we are only looking for peer-reviewed articles, let's also eliminate reviews from the search. Do so by selecting the red crossed-out checkmark across from the limiter which says Exclude this Reviews. Peer-reviewed journals contain reviews as well as articles, but these reviews do not count as peer-reviewed articles.

Now let's scroll through the results. Are they exactly on the topic we were looking for or do we need to change or add to our keywords?

Let's say that what we are really interested in is the environmental impact of electric vehicles. We haven't found a lot of those yet, so let's add a keyword.

Now comes the fun part. Don't search just yet.

Hover over the filter for peer-reviewed journals under the header Active filters. There is a lock that appears on the left of the filter and says "make this filter persistent throughout this session." Select this lock to keep the filter when you change the search terms. For now, lock all the filters.

Now let's add environmental to our keyword search.

Ok, now run the search by either pressing Enter or selecting the Search button.

The filters stayed with us as we changed our search terms. Awesome!

This doesn't only apply if you are just changing one word but also if you are completely changing your topic. And it is quite flexible.

Today, after this search on electric cars and the environment, you have another project you want to get started on. The project requires peer-reviewed articles, but the time frame for those articles isn't clear yet. So, before typing in the new keywords, just get rid of the date limiter altogether by hovering over the lock icon on the limiter and remove the persistent filter or eliminating the filter.

Now type in some keywords, like "water conservation", for the new search topic and press Enter. Only the peer-reviewed journals filter has remained persistent across the search, while the date limiter has been removed.

Awesome. Another cool feature is that if you do a new search in a new tab, these persistent filters will also be in the new tab. And this is cascading, so whatever the filters are in the previous tab will appear for a search in the next tab. This way, you can have multiple searches in different tabs and keep some or all of the limiters the same.

Locking filters and limiters can help you efficiently search for resources by eliminating the need to re-filter every time you search!

If you have any questions, please ask a librarian for help!

Endnotes

1. A lengthy discussion of how storytelling fits within the history and pedagogy of constructivist teaching can be found in chapter 4 of *Learning Through Storytelling in Higher Education: Using Reflection and Experience to Improve Learning*. The discussion on page 42 is particularly pertinent; Maxine Alterio and Janice McDrury, *Learning Through Storytelling in Higher Education: Using Reflection and Experience to Improve*

Learning (London: Taylor & Francis Group, 2003), 42, accessed August 3, 2020, ProQuest Ebook Central.
2. Steve Olusegun, "Constructivism Learning Theory: A Paradigm for Teaching and Learning," *Journal of Research & Method in Education* 5, no. 6 (2015): 66–70, http://iosrjournals.org/iosr-jrme/papers/Vol-5%20Issue-6/Version-1/I05616670.pdf.
3. "Simply put, narrative is the representation of an event or a series of events. 'Event' is the key word here, though some people prefer the word 'action.' Without an event or an action, you may have a 'description,' an 'exposition,' an 'argument,' a 'lyric,' some combination of these or something else altogether, but you won't have a narrative." H. Porter Abbot, *The Cambridge Introduction to Narrative*, 2nd ed. (New York: Cambridge University Press, 2008), 13.
4. Linda Harasim, *Learning Theory and Online Technologies* (New York: Routledge, 2001), 71.
5. Harasim, *Learning Theory*, 71.
6. "Persistent Filters and Limiters," Portland State University Library, YouTube video, June 13, 2019, https://www.youtube.com/watch?v=6ci8U_KYtfM.
7. "Persistent Filters and Limiters," Portland State University Library.
8. "In the constructivist model, the students are urged to be actively involved in their own process of learning"; Olusegun, "Constructivism Learning Theory," 68.
9. "Persistent Filters and Limiters," Portland State University Library.
10. Ibid.
11. Ibid.
12. Ibid.
13. Carlos León, "An Architecture of Narrative Memory," *Biologically Inspired Cognitive Architectures* 16 (2016): 31, https://doi.org/10.1016/j.bica.2016.04.002.
14. León, "An Architecture of Narrative Memory," 33.
15. "How to Meet WCAG (Quick Reference)," W3C Web Accessibility Initiative, last modified on June 4, 2019, https://www.w3.org/WAI/WCAG21/quickref/?versions=2.0.
16. "How to Meet WCAG (Quick Reference)," W3C Web Accessibility Initiative; WCAG 2.1.3.2: "When the sequence in which content is presented affects its meaning, a correct reading sequence can be programmatically determined"; 1.3.3: "Instructions provided for understanding and operating content do not rely solely on sensory characteristics of components such as shape, color, size, visual location, orientation, or sound"; 1.3.1 : "Information, structure, and relationships conveyed through presentation can be programmatically determined or are available in text."
17. Semantic Structure: Regions, Headings, and Lists. Web Accessibility in Mind, https://webaim.org/techniques/semanticstructure/.
18. "Persistent Filters and Limiters," Portland State University Library.

Bibliography

Abbot, H. Porter. *The Cambridge Introduction to Narrative*. 2nd ed. New York: Cambridge University Press, 2008.
Alterio, Maxine, and Janice McDrury. *Learning Through Storytelling in Higher Education: Using Reflection and Experience to Improve Learning*. London: Taylor & Francis Group, 2003. Accessed August 3, 2020. ProQuest Ebook Central.
Harasim, Linda. *Learning Theory and Online Technologies*. New York: Routledge, 2001.
León, Carlos. "An Architecture of Narrative Memory." *Biologically Inspired Cognitive Architectures* 16 (2016): 19–33. https://doi.org/10.1016/j.bica.2016.04.002.

Olusegun, Steve. "Constructivism Learning Theory: A Paradigm for Teaching and Learning." *Journal of Research & Method in Education* 5, no. 6 (2015): 66–70. http://iosrjournals.org/iosr-jrme/papers/Vol-5%20Issue-6/Version-1/I05616670.pdf.

Portland State University Library. "Persistent Filters and Limiters." YouTube video, June 13, 2019. https://www.youtube.com/watch?v=6ci8U_KYtfM.

Semantic Structure: Regions, Headings, and Lists. "Web Accessibility in Mind." Accessed December 13, 2020. https://webaim.org/techniques/semanticstructure/.

W3C Web Accessibility Initiative. "How to Meet WCAG (Quick Reference)." Accessed on December 13, 2020. https://www.w3.org/WAI/WCAG21/quickref/?versions=2.0.

Chapter 10

Using Existing Fandoms to Create Your Own Library Stories:

How a Harry Potter-Inspired Murder Mystery Introduced First-Year Students to the Library

Holly Jackson

The first week of classes at any university can be daunting—trying to find your way around campus, getting to know your roommate and other people on your floor, and trying to get used to being on your own. Or at least that's how it's going for me! It's finally Friday, and while I've got an 11:00 a.m. class, there's a Fall Fest event going on, too.

There are a *ton* of tables all around the Quad and heading up clear across campus to the Student Union. There are inflatables, food trucks, and I'm pretty sure every student organization you could ever imagine. One group even has cotton candy they're giving out!

I was kind of surprised to see a table for the library here. I mean, don't get me wrong, I'll definitely end up there, but they don't seem like they're really competing with the student orgs for my membership or anything. I got curious and dropped by, though, and they told me there's a Game Night tonight! An hour after they close, they're opening back up just for pizza and games. They should do this all the time! They said there are computer games, video games, and board games. Plus, they're trying a new Harry Potter-themed murder mystery. My roommate will love that—she's a huge Potterhead. I'm excited to see how they do this! I popped by on the first day of classes to print out my syllabi, and the library is huge. There's a massive open space on the second floor and I bet that's where they'll do the games.

Storytelling Goal

To introduce students to the library, both physically and virtually, and to test their knowledge of basic search skills.

Audience

Our primary audience was first-year and new-to-the-library students.[1]

Delivery

The original murder mystery was completed using printed posters hung up in various places around the library, along with the Aurasma app on students' phones.[2] Students would begin by self-identifying what Harry Potter "house" they belonged to (Gryffindor, Hufflepuff, Ravenclaw, or Slytherin). Then, they would start the activity by holding their phone, with the app open, over the house crest that they chose. Each one led to a different starting clue to split groups up. They would follow the clues around the library and then, after collecting the clues, solve a word search puzzle to get the answer to the "who did it?" question. If there were questions, I was stationed at the Information Desk during Game Night, or they could ask anyone at the Information Desk during separate instances of the game, as we had a guide to the game and clues at the Information Desk for staff to reference. During Game Night, we collected all completed word search final puzzles and drew winners from the correct answers. There were three prize boxes, each containing a gift card (either to the campus bookstore or a local restaurant), along with library giveaway items and a Harry Potter poster that I picked up from a local store.

You can see a shortened version of the Information Desk version of the instructions, including the game instructions and order of the clues in the appendix.

Theory

Going into the project, I drew on a lot of inspirations from various conference presentations and readings that I've engaged with related to gamification and game-based learning. While these sound similar, the two are different approaches to creating activities. Gamification is "the action or process of making something into or like a game; spec[ifically] the application of elements of game playing (such as point scoring, competition with others, etc.) to other areas of activity, typically to encourage engagement with a product or service."[3] This is what I consider the more common of the two. Using tools like Kahoot and other games where you tie in key information about your lessons that gain students points are examples of gamification. On the other hand, game-based learning is where the game itself *is* the lesson.[4] Gamification and game-based learning *are storytelling*. Using game elements and having students engage in these creative exercises where they put themselves in the middle of the lesson, in many cases, is also a way to support problem-based learning as students use their knowledge and skills to solve the problems presented in the game-based or gamified lessons.

For this particular activity, students become characters in the Harry Potter universe; they choose their Hogwarts house and become a character in their own right. It's essentially a form of role-playing to commit to that path and move along to solve the clues. Role-playing is also a great tool to help allow students to emerge themselves into a story and become more invested in the activity and the larger lessons being taught. From personal experience, some of the history lessons that have stayed with me the longest are the ones where I got to role-play in middle school: details about Ellis Island as I got to create a character and go through a mock Ellis Island experience with a full background story that I made up; details of important court cases as I got to serve as a lawyer on one side, presenting arguments in front of the class; learning about the various government offices by pretending to be an elected official representing a state of my choice. These sorts of activities deeply engage students and lead to more long-term learning and retention of information because they're more personally invested.

This activity serves as a sort of virtual tour and test of resources for students, hidden beneath the "murder mystery" façade. As students follow through the clues, they do things like find a book in the catalog and on the shelf, complete a simple database search, and look up a research guide, showing basic library research skills. They also navigated through the main two floors of the library, seeing the new 3D printer, the board game area, and other places they might not have explored yet. At any point, they're also told that it's okay to ask for help from a librarian, reinforcing the idea that it's okay to ask for help. So why frame all of this in a murder mystery? Really, because of personal interest in that medium. I love murder mysteries and have hosted several live-action murder mysteries with friends. The idea of a larger scale murder mystery combined with information literacy lessons was incredibly appealing on a personal level, and when I learned about augmented reality tools that were available, I loved the idea of making things connect to the concept of moving pictures shown in Harry Potter for clues. The inspiration is part Clue and part Harry Potter. If I would have run my revised game, I actually designed a modified Clue-inspired board to connect the dots a bit more easily on a handout for participants.

As I worked on the game elements, there were two theories that I kept in mind in particular: ARCS and Flow Theory. The ARCS Theory by John Keller refers to attention, relevance, confidence, and satisfaction. Are students actively connecting to the lesson and participating? How does this relate to the material begin taught or modeled? What control is given to the students and how is feedback provided? What praise and immediate application are students receiving? These are all questions related to this theory that I considered as this activity was being formed.[5] Flow Theory from Mihály Csíkszentmihályi examines that an activity is an "intrinsically rewarding task," has "clear goals and a sense of purpose," has "clear and immediate feedback," is a "match of challenge and skill," and has an "intense focus on the present moment."[6] Essentially, you want students to be "in the zone."[7] If things are too easy, students will get bored. On the other hand, if things are too hard, students will be frustrated. If you have a good flow, students will be in the zone and it will be successful.

Cultural Considerations

As I write this, J. K. Rowling is currently being called out for transphobic tweets on Twitter. It would be remiss of me to not begin by highlighting the fact that she is being looked at closely in terms of bias and that several people have written about the Harry Potter series, examining characters and storylines as analogies for J. K. Rowling's potential racist, antisemitic, and transphobic views. This calls into question whether it may be the best series to use in a similar activity. Some are arguing that the series is separate from the author, while others point out that you cannot fully remove the author from the stories they write. Creating an augmented reality activity, murder mystery or not, can be based on any story or situation you'd like, so take my specific example as an idea and feel free to create your own fun game! As this chapter's title suggests, you can use any existing fandom to create your own game and subsequent library stories.

In the future, I know I'd love to use any of Rick Riordan's series as inspiration, or any of the authors he highlights in his Rick Riordan Presents branch of publishing. The authors who publish under Rick Riordan Presents are all from underrepresented cultures and backgrounds telling stories from their mythologies and folklore, and they're all wonderful. Using other stories may also appeal to those students who are non-traditional and may not have grown up reading Harry Potter as I did. Using classic tales, folklore, mythology, or other stories that have been around for a while might be more inclusive for a wider variety of students to feel engaged. And while some may be unfamiliar with Harry Potter, others could be turned off by the magic in the tales, especially some students with more religious backgrounds whose beliefs do not condone magic. Examining your student population, especially their backgrounds and interests, can help you decide on the inspiration for your own activity.

Also, if you use a published work as your inspiration, be sure to take copyright into consideration. Because this activity has literary roots, I tried to stay with the familiar characters and ideas from the story, without delving into any purposeful copyright issues. The "victim" and "suspects" were randomly determined. I created a small bowl with folded up names of the more secondary but still recognizable characters from the books and selected one as the "victim" and then settled on "suspects" that that character might have actually interacted with in the story.

Practical Example

As you walk into the library, you see a large poster board on an easel with the Hogwarts House Crests on display. Next to it, there's a stack of folded handouts with instructions for the "Harry Potter Murder Mystery." Intrigued, you decide to start following along by downloading the Aurasma app and holding it over your chosen house crest. Grabbing your handout, you open it to the answer sheet and move to the first clue.

You start at the new 3D printer and find a wanted poster for "Sybill Trelawney," who looks a lot like Beth, who works at the Student Technology Assistance Center (a.k.a. the STAC). You open the Aurasma app again and hold it over the poster to play the video and get the first clue.

Your clue is:

- I'm seeing a lot of difficult times in your future.
- The grim does not lie—death is near.
- You can get some tea leaves of your own to read here, along with your next clue.
- Hint: On the first floor

INSTRUCTIONS:

1. Download the Aurasma app on your phone or tablet (Android or iPhone). First, create a free account, then go in to the main menu (☰), tap the magnifying glass, and search for WSUDunbarLibrary. Follow the page. It is the first option, seen here:

2. Once you're following WSUDunbarLibrary, click the ☐ button and hold your phone so that one of the house crests is in the center.

3. Begin following the clues. (A map is provided on the back of this handout.)
   - *If a character's video clue does not match their poster, simply move your phone or tablet away from the poster and then back onto the character to restart the clue.*

4. Once you've found all 10 clues, show the circulation desk (or Holly, at Game Night) to get the final answer sheet.

STOP BY THE INFORMATION DESK WITH ANY QUESTIONS!

If you complete the mystery, turn in your answer sheet to be entered to win one of several exciting prizes at Game Night - Friday, September 2 between 6:30-10:00pm!

VIDEO CLUES:

☆ All video clues are throughout the 1st and 2nd floors of Dunbar Library ☆

These are not in order of your search - write down the answers as you find the clues.

Bellatrix Lestrange Who was the first candidate on the left of the timeline in the display?	
Dolores Umbridge Who wrote this atlas?	
Gilderoy Lockhart What magical artifact was printed using this printer?	
Ginny Weasley What is the room where the clue takes you to called?	
Molly Weasley What hours will the Writing Center be in the Library on Sundays?	
Pomona Sprout What is the term on the planter that does not have a Wanted Poster?	
Rita Skeeter Who is the author of the stolen article?	
Rubeus Hagrid What game says that it will put a spell on you?	
Severus Snape What color was the potion on the left?	
Sybill Trelawney What is the name of the location where Trelawney tells you to go?	

Once you've finished the clues, show this to the Circulation Desk (or Holly at Game Night) for the final answer sheet!

Figure 10.1
Answer sheet

You head down to the Starbucks on the first floor and find a poster featuring "Rubeus Hagrid." You jot down "Starbucks" on the answer sheet and find that the next clue is:

- There's a storm comin', students.
- And we all best be ready when she does.
- Head to the area where ye can play with yer friends for yer next clue.
- Hint: In the Group Study area on the first floor

You know exactly what he's talking about, so you head to the board game collection in the Group Study area. There, you find the board game Curses, which answers the clue question of "What game says it will put a spell on you?" You write it down on the answer sheet and then find a poster of "Pomona Sprout," whose video clue tells you:

- Herbology is very important for young wizards to learn.
- How else can you learn to handle a mandrake or identify a poison?

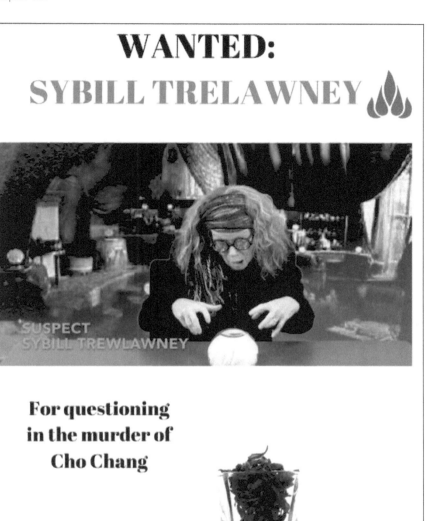

Figure 10.2
Sample poster

- These may not be Venomous Tentacluae, but you'll find your next clue with the plants at the top of the central stairs.
- Hint: One pot has your clue and the other has your next suspect.

Sure enough, you head to the top of the stairs and find your clue, the spell "Expecto Patronum," plus a poster of "Bellatrix Lestrange." Her video clue reveals:

- I love the smell of a good fight in the morning.
- With the election heating up, I've seen some information about the contenders.
- Find the Common Text Display for your next clue.
- Hint: Near the restrooms by the stairs

You head over to the display case and, after being slightly distracted by the Harry Potter House Cup Challenge bulletin board nearby, discover that the first candidate on the left of the timeline in the display is Woodrow Wilson. You jot that down in the answer sheet and find a poster for "Ginny Weasley," whose clue says:

- Lots of strange things have been going on here (and not just from Fred and George).
- You don't need a room of requirement all of the time…
- …but your next clue is in the room you and your mates can practice your skills in.
- Hint: Behind the Government Documents area

You're not 100 percent sure where this is, so you stop by the Information Desk to ask the librarian on duty where that might be. They're super helpful and tell you that's at the Presentation Practice Room and walk you back there. On your way, you jot down the name of the room on the answer sheet. Of course, once you're there, you notice a sign that says "Head to the laptop at the Bulletin Board for your next clue. Hint: Across from the 2nd floor bathroom." You sigh, since you were just there, and head back up for the clue. Near the laptop, you see a poster for "Rita Skeeter," which explains:

- One of my most popular pieces was a "Where are they now?" story about Hogwarts.
- Someone has ripped off my work and published it in a muggle magazine! Something called …*Time*.

- Look me up in your "Quick Search" and you'll find the name of the thief.
- Hint: Skeeter, Rita

You find that the library's webpage is already up on the laptop and that the Quick Search is the default search bar. Sweet! You're not sure where to start, so you type in the hint "Skeeter, Rita." Some things pop up, but you don't see anything that seems like it's that article. You decide to add that title from the first line, "Where are they now?" Ah-ha! Now it popped up and you see that the author, or thief, is Laura Stampler. You write that down on your answer sheet.

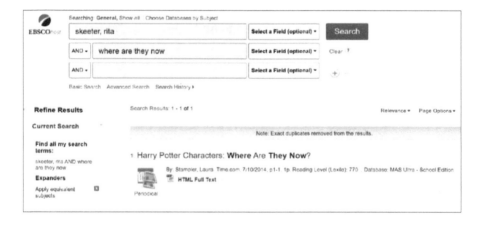

Figure 10.3
Search screenshot

You look over at the poster and find an envelope attached that says, "Read me to find out where to go after Rita." You open it up and find this direction: "You'll find your next clue at the closest catalog computer—near the yellow printer." You look up and notice that hanging above three printers near the computers are labels: "Green Printer," "Red Printer," and—bingo!—"Yellow Printer." You head that way and notice a computer against a column that says, "Catalog Computer." Next to it is a poster of "Dolores Umbridge," who says in her video clue:

- Things I love: cats, power, all things pink, cats.
- What I really need is an atlas to learn what cats are on my plates.
- I only want the best atlas! Find me *The Atlas of Cats of the World*!
- Hint: Search the catalog and then go to the Reference Section.

You type in "The Atlas of Cats of the World" into the catalog and it's the first result that shows up! You jot down the author, Dennis Kelsey-Wood, and head over to the Reference Section.

Figure 10.4
Catalog result

After a bit of searching, you find it and see a sign that says, "After you find the author, head to the laptop where the CaTS Desk used to be for your next clue. Hint: On the 2nd floor." You look over and see an empty desk area on the other side of the second floor with a laptop on a stand.

Heading over, you find a sign that says, "Use this computer to find your clue" and a poster for "Severus Snape," whose video tells you:

- If you insist on mediocrity in my class, the least you could do is look up the Chemistry Research Guide.
- Use the color to determine what color that potion was supposed to be.
- I don't expect you to understand, so let me make this clear—it should match the potion on the left in the picture.
- After that, your next clue can be found at the Information Desk.

You find the library's website open on the laptop and head to the area that says "Research Guides" and then in "Subject Guides" you find the one for Chemistry. Looking there, you see a picture with some test tubes and the one on the left is red. You write that down as the answer to the clue on your answer sheet and head over to the Information Desk.

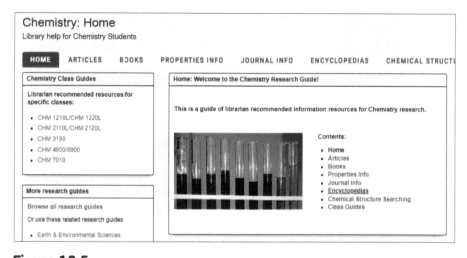

Figure 10.5
Chemistry Research Guide screenshot

At the Information Desk, you find a poster for "Molly Weasley," who mentions in her clue:

- My children aren't the only ones involved in shenanigans.
- Arthur has been doing more research into his muggle trinkets.
- You'll find your next clue in the Tutoring Area.
- Hint: Near the Music Scores

You head into the Tutoring Area and, sure enough, near the Music Scores you see a sign that has the hours the Writing Center is in the library. On Sundays, it looks like they're here from 2 to 7 p.m. You write that down on your answer sheet and find a poster for "Gilderoy Lockhart." It's your last poster! Phew! You watch his video, which says:

- You can now print miniature replicas of me!
- What a world we live in.
- Your next clue is at the printer that uses filament instead of ink.
- Hint: Find this in the STAC.

Oh! You know where this is! It's where you first started—the new 3D printer. You head back over there and notice that the magical artifact printed using the 3D printer was a copy of the Sorting Hat. You write that down.

VIDEO CLUE SHEET

This is the second page of the program that students are given to start.

☆ All video clues are throughout the 1st and 2nd floors of Dunbar Library ☆

These are not in order of your search—write down the answers as you find the clues.

Bellatrix Lestrange Who was the first candidate on the left of the timeline in the display?	Woodrow Wilson
Dolores Umbridge Who wrote this atlas?	Dennis Kelsey-Wood
Gilderoy Lockhart What magical artifact was printed using this printer?	Sorting Hat
Ginny Weasley What is the room where the clue takes you to called?	Presentation Practice Room
Molly Weasley What hours will the Writing Center be in the Library on Sundays?	2 to 7 pm
Pomona Sprout What is the term on the planter that does not have a Wanted Poster?	Expecto Patronum
Rita Skeeter Who is the author of the stolen article?	Laura Stampler
Rubens Hagrid What games says that it will put a spell on you?	Curses
Severus Snape What color was the potion on the left?	Red
Sybill Trelawney What is the name of the location where Trelawney tells you to go?	Starbucks

Once you've finished the clues, show this to the Circulation Desk (or Holly at Game Night) for the final answer sheet!

Figure 10.6
Completed answer sheet

Then, you head back downstairs to the Circulation Desk where the starting poster board was to get the final answer sheet. You sit down at one of the tables in the Group Study area to solve it:

146 Chapter 10

Harry Potter Murder Mystery Scavenger Hunt
☆Use your clue answers to solve the puzzle and figure out who did it!☆

Instructions:
Solve the clues below and then cross out the words in boxes in the puzzle on the back of the sheet. Once you're done, the remaining letters will spell out who murdered Cho Chang. Fill out the information at the bottom of the back of the sheet and turn it in when complete for a chance to win a prize during Game Night 2016.

Clues from the Scavenger Hunt:

Bellatrix Lestrange: ☐ ☐
Dolores Umbridge: ☐ ☐-☐
Gilderoy Lockhart: ☐ ☐
Ginny Weasley: ☐ ☐ ☐
Molly Weasley: _____
Pomona Sprout: ☐ ☐
Rita Skeeter: ☐ ☐
Rubeus Hagrid: ☐
Severus Snape: ☐
Sybill Trelawney: ☐

Clues from the Books:

The Potions professor: _____ ☐
The daughter of the editor of *The Quibbler*: ☐ _____
Head of Gryffindor House: ☐ _____
This man's impersonator was Barty Crouch, Jr.: _____ ☐ " ☐ " ☐
This produces a green flame for travel: ☐ _____
Harry's first crush: ☐ _____
An omen of death in the shape of a black dog: ☐
The least valued coin in the wizarding world: ☐
The acronym of Hermione's house elf organization: ☐
The wand extinguishing charm: ☐
The type of pet Harry chose to bring to Hogwarts: ☐
The magical instrument that channels a wizard's power: ☐
The eldest Weasley child: ☐

Figure 10.7
Clue sheet, part 1

D	O	W	O	O	D	R	O	W	L	S	B
E	P	A	N	S	E	S	P	E	W	O	I
P	A	T	R	O	N	U	M	O	R	R	L
R	F	W	N	E	N	L	U	N	A	T	L
A	L	A	O	W	I	L	S	O	N	I	D
C	O	N	I	S	S	U	S	M	M	N	O
T	O	D	T	N	O	X	E	A	I	G	O
I	P	L	A	U	R	A	S	D	N	H	W
C	O	M	T	M	O	O	R	E	E	A	Y
E	W	O	N	G	T	T	U	Y	R	T	E
O	D	O	E	R	U	C	C	E	V	M	S
W	E	D	S	I	N	H	B	E	A	R	L
L	R	Y	E	M	K	O	I	D	P	G	E
S	T	A	R	B	U	C	K	S	E	X	K
R	E	L	P	M	A	T	S	R	E	D	E

Enter any unused letters from the puzzle here:

The Murderer is: _____

Your Name: _____

Your Major: _____

WSU E-mail: _____

If you are not present at Game Night to win, you will be notified by e-mail if you have won.

Figure 10.8
Clue sheet, part 2

It takes a bit and a little Googling to help remember all of the book answers, but you figure it out—it was "Dolores Umbridge" who did it! You turn in the completed answer sheet and hope that you win the prize.

Chapter 10

Harry Potter Murder Mystery Scavenger Hunt

☆ Use your clue answers to solve the puzzle and figure out who did it! ☆

Instructions:
Solve the clues below and then cross out the words in boxes in the puzzle on the back of the sheet. Once you're done, the remaining letters will spell out who murdered Cho Chang. Fill out the information at the bottom of the back of the sheet and turn it in when complete for a chance to win a prize during Game Night 2016.

Clues from the Scavenger Hunt:

Bellatrix Lestrange: `Woodrow` `Wilson`
Dolores Umbridge: `Dennis` `Kelsey-Wood`
Gilderoy Lockhart: `Sorting Hat`
Ginny Weasley: `Presentation` `Practice` `Room`
Molly Weasley: 2 to 7 pm
Pomona Sprout: `Expecto` `Patronum`
Rita Skeeter: `Laura` `Stampler`
Rubeus Hagrid: `Curses`
Severus Snape: `Red`
Sybill Trelawney: `Starbucks`

Clues from the Books:

The Potions professor: `Severus` `Snape`
The daughter of the editor of *The Quibbler*: `Luna` `Lovegood`
Head of Gryffindor House: `Minerva` `McGonagall`
This man's impersonator was Barty Crouch, Jr.: `Alastor` " `Mad-Eye` " `Moody`
This produces a green flame for travel: `Floo` `Powder`
Harry's first crush: `Cho` `Chang`
An omen of death in the shape of a black dog: `Grim`
The least valued coin in the wizarding world: `Knut`
The acronym of Hermione's house elf organization: `SPEW`
The wand extinguishing charm: `Nox`
The type of pet Harry chose to bring to Hogwarts: `Owl`
The magical instrument that channels a wizard's power: `Wand`
The eldest Weasley child: `Bill`

Figure 10.9
Completed clue sheet, part 1

Using Existing Fandoms to Create Your Own Library Stories   149

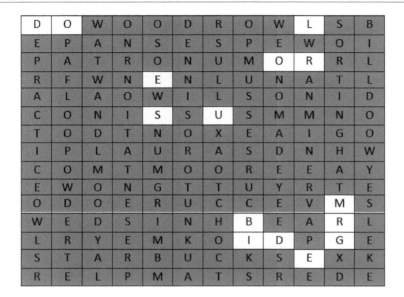

Figure 10.10
Completed clue sheet, part 2

Epilogue

After this first mystery experience was completed, I designed a revised version to run the following year, but due to budget and staffing constraints, we ended up putting things on hold. The revised card, shown in figure 6, was designed to look like a version of a Clue board for a more visually entertaining form. And instead of a puzzle, which proved to be the piece holding students up the most due to the time and effort required, I created a final guessing card, shown in figure 7, shaped like a chocolate frog box (a candy known in the Harry Potter world that you can actually purchase from some places).

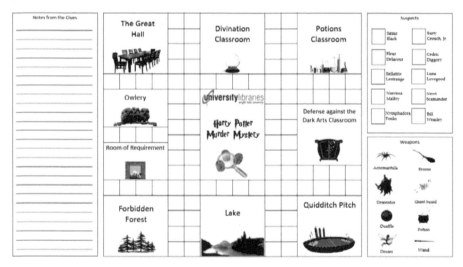

Figure 10.11
Draft answer sheet

Using Existing Fandoms to Create Your Own Library Stories 151

Figure 10.12
Draft final guessing card

Appendix

Harry Potter Murder Mystery Scavenger Hunt

INSTRUCTIONS

1. Students take one of the folded "Harry Potter Murder Mystery Scavenger Hunt" programs.

2. There are instructions on how to download the app in the program:

    a. Download the Aurasma app on an Android or Apple phone or tablet.

    b. Create a free account and then go into the main menu (). Then, click on the magnifying glass and search for WSUDunbarLibrary. Follow the page. It's the first option, seen here:

    c. Once they're following the WSUDunbarLibrary account, click the button and hold the phone over one of the house crests on the starting poster.

3. They will then follow the clues along the first and second floors of the Library, recording the answers in the program, starting with the house crest display next to the Circulation Desk near the programs.

4. If there are any questions, send them to the Information Desk if you're not comfortable directing them with the answer.

5. Once they finish recording the clues, they will drop by the Circulation Desk (or see Holly during Game Night) to receive a final answer sheet.

6. Once they've finished the final answer sheet, they submit it to be entered to win one of three prizes. Prizes are awarded during Game Night.

7. If any instructors would like attendance recorded for participation, they should send Holly a list of their students (holly.jackson@wright.edu) and she will contact them to let them know who participated in the activity.

FAQ

Q: What if I don't know anything about Harry Potter?

A: You're welcome to Google any Harry Potter related questions that you don't know, or to pair up with someone who is familiar with the books.

Q: What if I don't have an Apple or Android phone?

A: You are welcome to partner up with a friend or classmate to participate!

Q: What one is the WSU Dunbar Library account in my search results?

A: It's the very first option, seen here:

Q: How do I get back to the [ ] button?

A: If you have an **Apple** phone, hit the "Back" button at the top of the screen, then hit "Cancel" on the search and it will take you to the home page where the button is.

If you have an **Android** phone, it should be the center option at the bottom of the screen once you've followed WSUDunbarLibrary.

Q: What if the wrong person comes up when I hold the phone/tablet over a poster?

A: Simply move your phone away from the poster and then try it again. In most cases that we've tested, the right person will come up the second time if they didn't the first.

Q: What if I end up out of order?

A: That's okay! Simply go back to the clue where you ended up out of order to head back on the right track, or follow the clues back around to figure out what you've missed.

154 Chapter 10

Suspects

Rubeus Hagrid
Played by David Reyes
Location: Starbucks

Molly Weasley
Played by Maggie Perry
Location: Information Desk

Dolores Umbridge
Played by Michelle Brasseur
Location: Catalog Computer

Severus Snape
Played by Matthew Robinson
Sponsor: Residence Life & Housing
Location: Information Desk

Rita Skeeter
Played by Maureen Barry
Location: Laptop by the 2nd floor bulletin board

Ginny Weasley
Played by Jenn Weinle
Location: Common Text Display

Pomona Sprout
Played by Donna Bobb
Location: Board Games area

Sybill Trelawney
Played by Beth Anderson
Location: STAC 3D printer

Gilderoy Lockhart
Played by Matt Shreffler
Location: Tutoring area

Bellatrix Lestrange
Played by Kim Stephens
Sponsored by First Year Experience
Location: Planter @ top of 2nd floor stairs

Clue Order

BELLATRIX (PLANTER @ 2ND FLOOR STAIRS)
⬇
GINNY (COMMON TEXT DISPLAY)
⬇
PRESENTATION PRACTICE ROOM
⬇
RITA (2ND FLOOR BULLETIN BOARD)
⬇
UMBRIDGE (2ND FLOOR CATALOG COMPUTER)
⬇
CAT ATLAS (REF. SECTION)
⬇
SNAPE (OLD CATS DESK)
⬇
MOLLY (INFORMATION DESK)
⬇
LOCKHART (TUTOR TABLES)
⬇
TRELAWNEY (STAC 3D PRINTER)
⬇
HAGRID (STARBUCKS)
⬇
SPROUT (BOARD GAMES AREA)

Endnotes

1. You can see the original teaser video that we shared here: https://youtu.be/eQwc_gzxu5Y.
2. Important note: Aurasma no longer exists. Shortly after this activity, it changed to HP Studio, and then HP decided to drop augmented reality.
3. "gamification, n.," *Lexico*, June 2020, Oxford University, accessed July 17, 2020, https://www.lexico.com/en/definition/gamification.
4. For more on game-based learning theory, I recommend reading Jan L. Plass, Bruce D. Homer, and Charles K. Kinzer, "Foundations of Game-Based Learning," *Educational Psychologist* 50, no. 4 (2015): 258–83, https://doi.org/10.1080/00461520.2015.1122533.
5. Christopher Pappas, "Instructional Design Models and Theories," *eLearning Industry*, May 20, 2015, https://elearningindustry.com/arcs-model-of-motivation.
6. John Spencer, "What is Flow Theory?," YouTube, December 3, 2017, https://www.youtube.com/watch?v=iUsOCR1KKms.
7. Spencer, "What is Flow Theory?".

Bibliography

"gamification, n." *Lexico*. June 2020. Oxford University. Accessed June 17, 2020. https://www.lexico.com/en/definition/gamification.

Pappas, Christopher. "Instructional Design Models and Theories." *eLearning Industry*. May 20, 2015. https://elearningindustry.com/arcs-model-of-motivation.

Plass, Jan L., Bruce D. Homer, and Charles K. Kinzer. "Foundations of Game-Based Learning." *Educational Psychologist* 50, no. 4 (2015): 258–83. https://doi.org/10.1080/00461520.2015.1122533.

Spencer, John. "What is Flow Theory?" YouTube. December 3, 2017. https://www.youtube.com/watch?v=iUsOCR1KKms.

Biographies

About the Editors

Maria R. Barefoot is the online learning librarian at the University of Delaware. She became interested in the connection between storytelling and learning while pursuing her master of education degree from Indiana University of Pennsylvania. She has previously published in *Reference Services Review*, *Pennsylvania Libraries: Research and Practice*, and *The Library Assessment Cookbook*.

Sara Parme, MLIS, MBA, is the Project Director for the Appalachian College Association's Open and Affordable Resources Initiative and the Grants Coordinator of PA GOAL, Pennsylvania's open and affordable grants program. After working in academic libraries for nine years, thanks to the mentors and some wonderful people she's met along the way, her professional interests are virtual community building, project management, and not reinventing the wheel. She's always found the open and affordable community to be where the nice people are, and her professional aim is to surround herself with as many nice people as possible. In her previous job evaluations, she's often described as "informal" and "enthusiastic," two characteristics she's chosen to embrace as strengths when meeting new people and challenges. She is currently pursuing her PhD in Administration and Leadership Studies. Her dissertation focuses on status and incivility among academic library employees. She's a productivity geek and can have lengthy conversations about planners and focus apps.

Elin Woods is an independent researcher previously holding librarian posts at Saint Francis University and most recently at the Indiana University of Pennsylvania as a student success librarian. Her slightly unconventional path to libraries included time spent working at a newspaper and planning events before pursuing her MLIS from Clarion University. Since then, she has worked in both public and academic libraries, believing that they both have something to learn from one another. Her favorite way to tell stories is in the form of food, as she especially loves baking her way through historical Welsh and northern English cookbooks and the recipes she has from her grandmothers. When she's not whipping up something in the kitchen, you can find her exploring Appalachia or on the hunt for the perfect red lipstick.

About the Authors

Deanna Allred, MA, Utah State University, is a lecturer in the English Department. Deanna's work on Instagram communities has been published in the American Quilt Study Group *Uncoverings*. Her research interests include online communities, narrative, and composition studies.

L. E. Eames is an instruction librarian at the University of Colorado at Colorado Springs. He is the liaison librarian for government information and a handful of departments across the humanities. His research focuses on gender and information, information behavior and games, and social media performance. This project was completed while he was an MLIS student at the University of Washington Seattle iSchool and working on campus in the Government Publications, Maps, Microforms, and Newspapers unit of Suzzallo Library. Thanks to Kian Flynn, Cass Hartnett, and Anna Nelson for all the help and support in getting these guides off the ground!

Holly Jackson holds bachelor and master of art degrees in English literature from Wright State University and a master of library and information science degree from the University of Kentucky. She is the student success librarian at Mansfield University and has previously held humanities librarian positions at Tulane University and Wright State University. She's a huge fan of the *Harry Potter* series and loves incorporating game-based theory and gamification elements into the classroom and library in general. When she's not teaching or staffing a reference desk, you can find her partnering with the campus learning center or working on assessment practices.

Dunstan McNutt has an MA in history and an MLS from Indiana University Bloomington. He joined the Instruction Team at UTC in 2018 and, as a generalist, seeks to facilitate and support student research across disciplines. Dunstan's research interests include learner engagement within the realm of information literacy, teaching with primary sources, and diversity and inclusion work in academic librarianship.

Gerald Natal has a BFA from Bowling Green State University and a library degree from Kent State University. His thirty-plus years of library experience ranges from driving a bookmobile for a public library system to working in a correctional institution library to currently providing reference and instruction in an academic setting. A research interest in outreach has led to presentations and publications on reference services, comics and graphic novels in libraries, and library services to military-affiliated students.

Alexis L. Pavenick, PhD, MLIS, MA, MPhil, taught humanities and social sciences at the college level for about seventeen years before becoming a humanities librarian. In her current position as senior assistant librarian for the English Department and the programs of classics and comparative world literature at California State University, Long Beach, she provides library instruction sessions, consultations, online tutorials, and collection development alongside her committee work and research projects.

Megan Smith is currently the technical services librarian at East Stroudsburg University and department chair. Before starting at ESU in 2015, Megan was a cataloging librarian at the Franklin Township Public Library in Somerset, NJ. Prior to becoming a librarian, Megan worked primarily in museums in various roles, including the Metropolitan Museum of Art. She lives in NJ with her family.

Katie Strand, MLS, Utah State University, is a first-year experience librarian. Her primary role is coordinating the library's first-year programming efforts, including the face-to-face and online composition program, first-year orientation, and other first-year partnerships. Along with her first-year focus, Katie also serves as the library liaison to the Environment and Society, Watershed Sciences, and Wildland Resources departments.

Alex Sundt, MLS, Utah State University, is the web services librarian. Alex's work is focused on applying UX tools and techniques to better understand library users and improve the design of library user experiences. In addition, he provides reference and instruction and serves as the liaison to computer science and several departments in the Huntsman School of Business. His scholarship has been published in *Weave: Journal of Library User Experience* and the *Journal of Web Librarianship*. In addition to web services, Alex's interests include service design, scholarly communication, and the intersections between online services and library instruction.

Anders Tobiason is the multimedia development and user experience librarian at Boise State University Albertsons Library. He teaches information literacy sessions both online and in-person, creates multimedia learning objects, thinks a lot about user experience and access, and works on diversity, equity, and inclusion initiatives. He holds a Bachelor of Music degree from the University of Massachusetts, Amherst, and an MA and PhD in music theory as well as an MA in library and information science from the University of Wisconsin, Madison. His research interests include accessibility and equity in library instruction, critical information literacy, multimedia development, critical discourse analysis of library instructional standards and materials, and social media use in library instruction.

Dr. Harrison Wick is the special collections librarian and university archivist at Indiana University of Pennsylvania (IUP) in Indiana, Pennsylvania. As a member of the library faculty, he also serves at the reference desk, teaches bibliographic instruction, and provides collection development for several disciplines. Dr. Wick recently earned his doctorate in administration and leadership studies from IUP. His dissertation focused on Civil War leadership using the study of logistics from the Battle of Gettysburg as a case study of historical research. He also earned graduate degrees in history and library science from Indiana University in Bloomington, Indiana, and an undergraduate degree in history from Washington College in Chestertown, Maryland.

Allyson Wind is currently the electronic resources librarian at East Stroudsburg University and liaison librarian for ESU's Department of Education. Before starting at ESU in 2016, Allyson was the web services librarian at the Geisinger Commonwealth School of Medicine (GCSOM—formerly TCMC). She was also a librarian at the Kingston City Library and the Phoenicia Public Library in New York's Hudson Valley. Prior to becoming a librarian, Allyson taught in various school districts in Northeastern Pennsylvania as a substitute teacher. She lives just outside of Scranton with her husband and three rescue cats.

Rachel Wishkoski, MA, MLIS, Utah State University, is a reference and instruction librarian. She holds an MA in ethnomusicology from Ohio State University, and an MLIS from the University of Washington. In her role as a reference and instruction librarian at Utah State University, she serves as the liaison to several academic departments. Rachel's work has been published in *portal: Libraries and the Academy*, *Communications in Information Literacy*, the *Journal of the Association for Information Science and Technology*, and the *Journal of Library & Information Services in Distance Learning*. Her research interests include information literacy pedagogy and faculty development initiatives.

Kathryn Yelinek works as a research & scholarly publishing librarian at Bloomsburg University of Pennsylvania, where she is the librarian for anthropology; English; environmental, geographical, and geological sciences; political science; and psychology. When not in the library, she likes to keep her eyes on the sky: she's a birdwatcher as well as a stargazer.